AIDS
OPPOSING VIEWPOINTS®

Other Books of Related Interest

AIDS

OPPOSING VIEWPOINTS®

Tamara L. Roleff, *Book Editor*

Daniel Leone, *President*
Bonnie Szumski, *Publisher*
Scott Barbour, *Managing Editor*
Helen Cothran, *Senior Editor*

OPPOSING
VIEWPOINTS®
SERIES

GREENHAVEN
PRESS®

THOMSON
—————————*—————————™
GALE

San Diego • Detroit • New York • San Francisco • Cleveland
New Haven, Conn. • Waterville, Maine • London • Munich

For more information, contact
Greenhaven Press
27500 Drake Rd.
Farmington Hills, MI 48331-3535
Or you can visit our Internet site at http://www.gale.com

LIBRARY OF CONGRESS CATALOGING-IN-PUBLICATION DATA

AIDS / Tamara L. Roleff, book editor.
 p. cm. — (Opposing viewpoints)
Includes bibliographical references and index.
ISBN 0-7377-1136-1 (lib. bdg. : alk. paper) —
ISBN 0-7377-1135-3 (pbk. : alk. paper)
 1. AIDS (Disease)—Public opinion. I. Roleff, Tamara L., 1959– . II. Opposing
viewpoints series (Unnumbered)
RA643.8 .A42 2003
362.1'969792—dc21
                  2002070611

Printed in the United States of America

"Congress shall make no law... abridging the freedom of speech, or of the press."

First Amendment to the U.S. Constitution

The basic foundation of our democracy is the First Amendment guarantee of freedom of expression. The Opposing Viewpoints Series is dedicated to the concept of this basic freedom and the idea that it is more important to practice it than to enshrine it.

Contents

**Chapter 3: How Can the Spread of AIDS Be
Controlled?**

Why Consider Opposing Viewpoints?

"The only way in which a human being can make some approach to knowing the whole of a subject is by hearing what can be said about it by persons of every variety of opinion and studying all modes in which it can be looked at by every character of mind. No wise man ever acquired his wisdom in any mode but this."

John Stuart Mill

In our media-intensive culture it is not difficult to find differing opinions. Thousands of newspapers and magazines and dozens of radio and television talk shows resound with differing points of view. The difficulty lies in deciding which opinion to agree with and which "experts" seem the most credible. The more inundated we become with differing opinions and claims, the more essential it is to hone critical reading and thinking skills to evaluate these ideas. Opposing Viewpoints books address this problem directly by presenting stimulating debates that can be used to enhance and teach these skills. The varied opinions contained in each book examine many different aspects of a single issue. While examining these conveniently edited opposing views, readers can develop critical thinking skills such as the ability to compare and contrast authors' credibility, facts, argumentation styles, use of persuasive techniques, and other stylistic tools. In short, the Opposing Viewpoints Series is an ideal way to attain the higher-level thinking and reading skills so essential in a culture of diverse and contradictory opinions.

In addition to providing a tool for critical thinking, Opposing Viewpoints books challenge readers to question their own strongly held opinions and assumptions. Most people form their opinions on the basis of upbringing, peer pressure, and personal, cultural, or professional bias. By reading carefully balanced opposing views, readers must directly confront new ideas as well as the opinions of those with whom they disagree. This is not to simplistically argue that everyone who reads opposing views will—or should—change his or her opinion. Instead, the series enhances readers' understanding of their own views by encouraging confrontation with opposing ideas. Careful examination of others' views can lead to the readers' understanding of the logical inconsistencies in their own opinions, perspective on why they hold an opinion, and the consideration of the possibility that their opinion requires further evaluation.

Evaluating Other Opinions

To ensure that this type of examination occurs, Opposing Viewpoints books present all types of opinions. Prominent spokespeople on different sides of each issue as well as well-known professionals from many disciplines challenge the reader. An additional goal of the series is to provide a forum for other, less known, or even unpopular viewpoints. The opinion of an ordinary person who has had to make the decision to cut off life support from a terminally ill relative, for example, may be just as valuable and provide just as much insight as a medical ethicist's professional opinion. The editors have two additional purposes in including these less known views. One, the editors encourage readers to respect others' opinions—even when not enhanced by professional credibility. It is only by reading or listening to and objectively evaluating others' ideas that one can determine whether they are worthy of consideration. Two, the inclusion of such viewpoints encourages the important critical thinking skill of objectively evaluating an author's credentials and bias. This evaluation will illuminate an author's reasons for taking a particular stance on an issue and will aid in readers' evaluation of the author's ideas.

It is our hope that these books will give readers a deeper understanding of the issues debated and an appreciation of the complexity of even seemingly simple issues when good and honest people disagree. This awareness is particularly important in a democratic society such as ours in which people enter into public debate to determine the common good. Those with whom one disagrees should not be regarded as enemies but rather as people whose views deserve careful examination and may shed light on one's own.

Thomas Jefferson once said that "difference of opinion leads to inquiry, and inquiry to truth." Jefferson, a broadly educated man, argued that "if a nation expects to be ignorant and free . . . it expects what never was and never will be." As individuals and as a nation, it is imperative that we consider the opinions of others and examine them with skill and discernment. The Opposing Viewpoints Series is intended to help readers achieve this goal.

David L. Bender and Bruno Leone,
Founders

Greenhaven Press anthologies primarily consist of previously published material taken from a variety of sources, including periodicals, books, scholarly journals, newspapers, government documents, and position papers from private and public organizations. These original sources are often edited for length and to ensure their accessibility for a young adult audience. The anthology editors also change the original titles of these works in order to clearly present the main thesis of each viewpoint and to explicitly indicate the opinion presented in the viewpoint. These alterations are made in consideration of both the reading and comprehension levels of a young adult audience. Every effort is made to ensure that Greenhaven Press accurately reflects the original intent of the authors included in this anthology.

Introduction

"The idea that HIV causes AIDS is an idea that has not been proven to be correct or true."
—Christine Maggiore, ABC News 20/20, *August 24, 2001*

"HIV causes AIDS. It is unfortunate that a few vocal people continue to deny the evidence."
—Durban Declaration, Nature, *July 6, 2000*

The Centers for Disease Control and Prevention (CDC) announced in June 1981 that it had identified a new disease—now known as AIDS—that was killing people with illnesses that were normally held in check by the body's immune system. The CDC believed that AIDS was an infectious disease because the first cases were grouped in geographic clusters in New York, San Francisco, and Los Angeles. Researchers discovered that the disease was transmitted sexually; later it was determined that AIDS was also spread through contaminated blood and from mother to infant.

In April 1984, Robert Gallo, an American AIDS researcher with the National Institutes of Health (NIH), announced to great fanfare that he had found the probable cause of AIDS, a retrovirus called the human immunodeficiency virus (HIV). A French researcher, Luc Montagnier of the Pasteur Institute in Paris, also claimed that he had discovered the virus that causes AIDS, and the two men are credited as being the codiscoverers of HIV.

HIV is a retrovirus, a smaller type of virus that was relatively unknown when it was discovered. The outer membrane surrounding HIV is composed of human cells; this makes it very difficult for the body's immune system to fight HIV as it cannot easily distinguish HIV from normal cells. Gallo and Montagnier theorized that HIV attacks its host's T4 cells (which coordinate the body's response against an infection). When T4 cells are disabled, the immune system is not able to protect the body, and the host is open to attack by opportunistic infections.

Not everyone agrees that HIV causes AIDS, however.

Dozens of scientists, researchers, and former AIDS activists are questioning the science behind the HIV hypothesis and AIDS research itself. Some of these AIDS "dissenters" even dispute the existence of AIDS. Peter Duesberg, a renowned microbiologist who is a pioneer in retrovirus research, argues that diseases were suddenly diagnosed as AIDS solely because HIV was present in the patient's bloodstream. If the patient did not have HIV, then the disease was "diagnosed by its old name and blamed on conventional chemical or microbial causes." For example, he said if a patient had tuberculosis and HIV, the patient was diagnosed with AIDS. But if the patient had tuberculosis without HIV, he was diagnosed as having just tuberculosis. Even Thabo Mbeki, the president of South Africa, has joined the AIDS dissenters. At an international conference on AIDS held in Durban, South Africa, in July 2000, Mbeki told a stunned crowd, "It seemed to me that we could not blame everything on a single virus."

Many AIDS dissenters have their own theory of what causes AIDS: The consumption of recreational and pharmaceutical drugs, such as cocaine, nitrate inhalants known as poppers, amphetamines, heroin, LSD, marijuana, PCP, and others. According to Duesberg, almost every early AIDS patient was a homosexual who used drugs as a sexual stimulant or a heterosexual drug addict who injected drugs intravenously. "Drugs seemed to be the most plausible explanation for the near-perfect restriction of AIDS to these risk groups because drug consumption is their most specific, common denominator," Duesberg maintains in his book *Inventing the AIDS Virus.* He explains that these recreational drugs are toxic, but it takes long-term drug use to build up toxicity in the body, much as long-term smoking causes lung cancer or emphysema. He also argues that while it may take ten years for heroin, amphetamines, or cocaine to build up enough toxicity in the body to cause AIDS, it only takes a year for an extremely toxic AIDS drug such as AZT to cause AIDS.

AIDS researchers reject the dissenters' view that recreational drug use causes AIDS. They point out that people had been using recreational drugs for many years without contracting AIDS. Indeed, they argue that the opportunistic infections commonly seen in AIDS patients were rare until

HIV was discovered. Additional proof that HIV, not recreational drug use, causes AIDS is a 1993 study published in *Lancet* magazine, which followed 715 homosexual men—365 who were HIV-positive—for more than eight years. The researchers found that 136 of the HIV-positive men developed AIDS, while none of the men who were not HIV-positive did, despite the fact that they all took poppers and other recreational drugs. The researchers also refute the claim that AIDS drugs such as AZT cause AIDS. They point out that many people who have contracted AIDS never ingested anti-AIDS drugs. In addition, the National Institute of Allergy and Infectious Diseases (NIAID) maintains that AZT has helped people with HIV and AIDS: "AZT given as single-drug therapy delayed, for a year or two, the onset of AIDS-related illnesses."

The NIAID, the CDC, and other government health organizations, as well as almost every scientist and AIDS researcher accepts the hypothesis that HIV causes AIDS. They assert that HIV is found in every patient who develops AIDS, the virus has been isolated and grown in a test tube, and the isolated virus has been transferred (albeit accidentally via needle-sticks) to uninfected hosts. These conditions meet every one of Koch's postulates, a set of tenets that have been used for more than a century to determine the cause of a disease. "Other viral infections, bacterial infections, sexual behavior patterns and drug abuse patterns do not predict who develops AIDS," contends the NIAID. The Institute adds that AIDS develops in people with diverse backgrounds whose only commonality is that they all have been infected with HIV.

Whether AIDS is a real disease, and if so, what causes it, are among the issues debated in *AIDS: Opposing Viewpoints*, which contains the following chapters: What Is the State of the Global AIDS Epidemic? What Policies Should Be Adopted for HIV Testing? How Can the Spread of AIDS Be Controlled? How Should AIDS Be Treated? The authors in this anthology present a wide range of opinions on the many controversies surrounding the prevention, diagnosis, and treatment of this disease.

CHAPTER 1

What Is the State of the Global AIDS Epidemic?

Chapter Preface

While the numbers of Americans contracting AIDS and dying of the disease are falling, many commentators assert that AIDS is spreading rapidly throughout the rest of the world, especially in Africa and Asia. David Ho, director of the Aaron Diamond AIDS Research Center and *Time*'s 1996 Man of the Year for his work with AIDS, predicts that "the global AIDS epidemic will get much worse before it gets any better." Officials at the Joint United Nations Programme on HIV/AIDS (UNAIDS) estimate that 40 million people worldwide are living with AIDS, with about 35.6 million of them in Asia and Africa.

The average annual cost of drugs to fight AIDS is $12,000–$15,000, way beyond the means of most Africans and Asians. African leaders and AIDS activists have pleaded with the pharmaceutical companies that manufacture the AIDS drugs to donate the drugs—or sell them at deeply discounted prices—so that AIDS victims in the developing world have a chance at survival. Even if the drug companies slashed the price of their drugs to $2 per day, however, they would still be too expensive for most Africans.

The drug companies, most of which are based in the United States and Europe, argue that the high drug prices are necessary in order to finance research on other drugs. They also claim that AIDS victims in poor countries do not have adequate health support facilities to monitor drug treatments. Without proper scientific support, Africans with AIDS will not be able to adhere to the strict drug regimen that keeps AIDS at bay. Moreover, if the drugs are not taken properly, the AIDS virus can easily mutate and develop a resistance to the drugs, resulting in drug-resistant strains of HIV.

There is no question that access to AIDS drugs could save millions of lives if the drug regimen is followed correctly. The authors in the following chapter debate whether Africans will one day have improved access to and the ability to use correctly such drugs. To be sure, Africa's failure to do so could threaten the rest of the world.

"The AIDS epidemic is becoming increasingly complex. . . . More people are living with HIV/AIDS than ever before, and significant disparities exist across age and race."

The American AIDS Epidemic Is Still a Concern

Regina Aragón, Jennifer Kates, Liberty Green, and Tina Hoff

Although new infections of HIV/AIDS have declined in recent years in the United States, many Americans view the AIDS epidemic as one of the most important health problems facing the country, assert Regina Aragón, Jennifer Kates, Liberty Green, and Tina Hoff in the following viewpoint. The authors maintain that more Americans are infected with HIV than ever before. In addition, new HIV infections are having a disproportionate impact on minorities and young adults. According to the authors, many Americans do not believe their government is doing enough to fight the AIDS epidemic. Aragón was a member of Bill Clinton's Presidential Advisory Council on HIV/AIDS; Kates, Green, and Hoff are all researchers with the Kaiser Family Foundation.

As you read, consider the following questions:
1. When did the Centers for Disease Control and Prevention issue its first warning about AIDS, according to the authors?
2. According to Aragón and her colleagues, how many Americans know someone who is either living with AIDS or has died from the disease?

Regina Aragón, Jennifer Kates, Liberty Green, and Tina Hoff, *The AIDS Epidemic at 20 Years: The View from America: A National Survey of Americans on HIV/AIDS*, 2001. Copyright © 2001 by Henry J. Kaiser Family Foundation. Reproduced with permission.

On June 5, 1981, the U.S. Centers for Disease Control and Prevention (CDC) issued its first warning about a relatively rare form of pneumonia among a small group of young gay men in Los Angeles, which was later determined to be AIDS-related. Since that time, more than 750,000 cases of AIDS have been reported in the U.S. and almost half a million Americans have died of the disease. Of the more than 36 million individuals worldwide estimated to be living with HIV/AIDS, approximately 95% live in the developing world—a full 70% in sub-Saharan Africa alone.

During this twenty-year period, there has been a great deal of progress in the fight against AIDS. New infections in the U.S. have declined dramatically, and there are signs that new infections in sub-Saharan Africa may be stabilizing. The more widespread use of antiretroviral drugs has also contributed to fewer new AIDS cases and AIDS-related deaths.

Despite this progress, critical challenges remain. The AIDS epidemic is becoming increasingly complex. Proven prevention programs are not reaching everyone in need. More people are living with HIV/AIDS than ever before, and significant disparities exist across age and race. For example, while African Americans and Latinos represent 12% and 13% of the U.S. population, they represent 47% and 19% of reported cases, respectively. An estimated half of all new infections in the U.S. are among those under the age of 25. In addition, the high cost of HIV care presents significant barriers to access for people with HIV/AIDS in the United States, many of whom are not in regular care, and treatment is not available to the vast majority of those living with HIV/AIDS in the developing world. And though progress is steady, we are still years away from developing an effective vaccine. . . .

Americans' Perception of the Epidemic

The American public continues to view HIV/AIDS as one of the most urgent health problems facing the nation (26%), ranking it second only to cancer (35%). The proportion, however, who view AIDS as the number one health problem facing the nation has declined, from 44% in 1995 to 26% in 2000.

Globally, Americans see AIDS as the most urgent health issue with more than one-third (37%) ranking it as number one, followed by cancer. Concern also hits close to home, with more than one-third (37%) expressing personal concern about becoming infected, and more than four in ten (43%) saying that they personally know someone who is either living with HIV/AIDS or has died of AIDS. Two in five (40%) say that AIDS is a serious problem for people they know and almost one-quarter (23%) say that the problem of AIDS is a more urgent one in their local communities than a few years ago.

The sense of urgency regarding AIDS is particularly strong among racial and ethnic minority groups in the U.S., perhaps reflecting the disproportionate and growing impact of HIV on people of color. For example, substantially higher proportions of African Americans (41%) and Latinos (40%) view AIDS as the number one health problem facing the nation, compared with whites (23%). African Americans (70%) and Latinos (64%) are also much more likely than whites (44%) to feel that HIV/AIDS is a more urgent problem now than it was a few years ago. But even among minority Americans, the proportion ranking AIDS as the number one health problem facing the nation has declined over the past five years.

Parents of children and young adults appear to be acutely aware of the growing impact of HIV on America's youth. Nearly three-quarters (71%) of parents of children under age 21 report being either "very" or "somewhat" concerned about their son or daughter becoming infected with HIV. The majority (52%) of 18 to 24 year olds also say they are personally concerned about becoming infected with HIV.

Americans' Knowledge and Information Needs

Nearly all Americans are aware that HIV can be transmitted through unprotected intercourse (99%), the sharing of intravenous (IV) needles (99%), and unprotected oral sex (91%). Fewer than half (42%), however, know that having another sexually transmitted disease (STD) increases a person's risk for HIV. In addition, even after years of public education, unwarranted fears of infection through casual contact persist.

For example, one in five (22%) Americans incorrectly believes that sharing a drinking glass can transmit HIV, or are unsure about the risk of this activity. Sixteen percent believe that touching a toilet seat can transmit HIV or are unsure about the risk. Unfortunately, such views contribute to discrimination and stigma, which can interfere with public health efforts to encourage early testing and care.

Americans Remain Concerned About AIDS

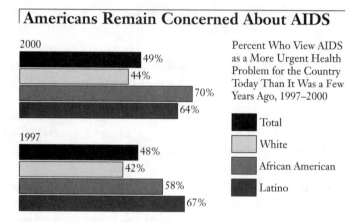

Regina Aragón et al., *The AIDS Epidemic at 20 Years: A National Survey of Americans on HIV/AIDS,* 2001.

Americans' knowledge about clinical issues related to the disease is uneven. For example, although 86% of all Americans know that there are drugs available that can lengthen the lives of people living with HIV/AIDS, less than half (43%) of all Americans are aware that treatments are available to prevent mother-to-child transmission of HIV. They are, however, eager for more information, particularly about how to talk to children about AIDS and about HIV testing.

Policy Issues

Americans believe that many key stakeholders are not doing enough to fight the AIDS epidemic. Two-thirds (66%) say the federal government is not doing enough, and a majority say that their state or local governments (59%) and schools (51%) are not doing enough. Americans also believe that private sector efforts and those of parents should be strengthened.

A majority of Americans (55%) say that the federal government is spending too little money on AIDS, with one-quarter (25%) saying spending is about right and 5% saying spending is too much. Americans strongly support federal government activities focusing on AIDS prevention and education (86%), research to find a vaccine (83%), and treatment and care (75%). Majorities support policies designed to increase access to sterile syringes among injection drug users and school-based sex education about HIV/AIDS. For example, 58% support needle exchange programs, which offer clean needles to IV drug users in exchange for used ones, and 97% believe that high school sex education should address how HIV and other STDs are spread.

Support for efforts to address the global pandemic is also strong. Two-thirds (66%) of Americans support U.S. spending on AIDS in sub-Saharan Africa, compared to 29% who oppose such spending. Forty percent say that the U.S. government should be doing more in this region of the world; 33% say the U.S. government is doing the right amount and 13% say the government should be doing less. Americans favor U.S. financial assistance in sub-Saharan Africa in the areas of prevention (77%), treatment and care (75%) and reducing foreign debt (65%). A large majority (81%) of Americans also believe that pharmaceutical companies should be willing to cut drug prices in developing countries to help in the fight against AIDS.

Future Challenges

As the AIDS epidemic grows more complex and continues to take a disproportionate toll on racial and ethnic minority populations, U.S. policymakers will be faced with a number of critical challenges. These include: how to finance and ensure equal access to HIV care and treatment; how to take full advantage of proven HIV prevention programs that often deal with the politically controversial and socially difficult issues of sexuality and drug use; and how to determine the appropriate role of the U.S. in global efforts.

The findings from this survey indicate that a majority of Americans continue to support increased federal spending on AIDS in the U.S. and in sub-Saharan Africa and support a range of HIV-related policies. Americans continue to view AIDS as one of the most important health problems facing the U.S. today. There are signs, however, of some decline in public concern on certain fronts. This is true among those hardest hit by the epidemic, minority Americans, as well as the general public. In addition, knowledge about HIV/AIDS remains somewhat uneven. This complex picture points to a new set of challenges for policymakers, public health officials, and other stakeholders as they seek to address the epidemic in its third decade.

"The American AIDS epidemic is over."

The Extent of the American AIDS Epidemic Is Exaggerated

Michael Fumento

Michael Fumento has written extensively on AIDS and is the author of *The Myth of Heterosexual AIDS*. He argues in the following viewpoint that the extent of the AIDS epidemic in the United States has been exaggerated. In fact, the number of new AIDS cases and deaths reported annually has been dropping steadily since 1994, as have the cases reported by heterosexuals, teens, children, and rural residents. The one segment of the population that is truly suffering from AIDS is minorities, a trend the author predicted in his book published in 1993.

As you read, consider the following questions:
1. What is the modern definition of an epidemic, as cited by Fumento?
2. What percentage of AIDS cases is comprised of teens, according to the Centers for Disease Control and Prevention?
3. Approximately how many people died of AIDS in 2000, as cited by the author?

Michael Fumento, "The Band Plays On: Good News on AIDS—Why the Silence?" *American Spectator*, October 2001. Copyright © 2001 by Gilder Publishing. Reproduced with permission.

If I ever decide I need to get blood from a turnip, I'm calling on the Centers for Disease Control (CDC) and Prevention and their friends in the media.

Why? For almost fifteen years now they have performed the incredible feat of exaggerating the AIDS epidemic in every possible way, to make it more politically correct and bring more money into federal health agency coffers.

No matter how overblown their previous predictions and assertions prove, no matter how good the news to the contrary, they always find a way to make the end of the world seem just around the corner.

Consider the following August [2001] headlines: "U.S. AIDS Findings Cause Concern" (*Associated Press*); "AIDS Maintaining Its Grip in U.S." (*San Francisco Chronicle*); "Ill Omen: Decline of AIDS Levels Off" (*Atlanta Journal and Constitution*); "Resurgence Feared After Drop in AIDS Deaths" (*USA Today*); "A 'Chilling Portrait' of Failure to Prevent AIDS" (*Los Angeles Times*).

The Epidemic Is Over

What you should have read was that the American AIDS epidemic is over.

That's right. To paraphrase a famous Monty Python sketch, "This epidemic is no more! It has ceased to be! It's expired and gone to meet its maker! This is a late epidemic. It's a stiff! Bereft of life, it rests in peace! It's run down the curtain and joined the choir invisible! This . . . is an ex-epidemic!"

By the modern definition, an epidemic is a disease that surpasses an expected level of cases for a certain length of time. Since previously there were no reported AIDS cases, AIDS certainly qualified as an epidemic from 1981. In 1993 it peaked at 106,000 new cases, then declined yearly, and has now leveled off at a considerably lower rate of about 40,000 cases a year. AIDS is still with us, but it is epidemic no more.

Obviously we're still getting 40,000 more cases yearly than we'd like. But it's a safe bet that diseases without a cure that are spread and contracted overwhelmingly by people who put themselves knowingly at risk will continue to persist.

And here's some good news that anyone can access in the 2000 CDC HIV/AIDS annual report (available at: http://

www.cdc.gov/hiv/stats/hasr1202.htm), but that nobody in the media has bothered to tell you:

- Forget the heterosexual AIDS epidemic. The category of those who so much as claim to have gotten the disease this way comprises over 90 percent of the population but only 11 percent of AIDS cases. In 1993, 9,570 such cases were reported. By 1999 it was down to 7,139 and in 2000 it fell further, to 6,530.
- Forget the teenage epidemic. Teen cases comprised less than one percent of the total in 2000, or 342. This is down from 588 cases in 1993. True, former CDC chief and current Surgeon General David Satcher did tell a credulous Juan Williams at NPR in early July 2001 that "the median age for women getting AIDS today is about 16." Actually, the median according to the CDC annual report is the 30–34 year-old range. Could he have meant HIV infections, the earliest stage of the disease? No, the median for those is also the 30–34 year-old range.
- Forget the "rural AIDS explosion." Rural cases comprised 14 percent of the total in 2000, or 3,061 in number. This is down from 5,809 cases in 1993.
- Forget all that "leading cause of death" stuff. AIDS fell off the CDC top 15 list back in 1998. AIDS deaths have declined from a high of over 50,000 in 1995 to about 12,000 per year in 2001. Fewer people died of AIDS last year than any year since 1985.
- Childhood AIDS is disappearing. The total of pediatric AIDS cases last year was less than 200, compared to 959 in 1993.

The Numbers Are Declining

What about this talk of resurgence? In August 2001, the outgoing director of the CDC's National Center for HIV, STD [sexually transmitted diseases], and TB [tuberculosis] Prevention, Helene Gayle, told reporters that infections in heterosexual women are increasing more rapidly than any other group. But the CDC's numbers show reported female HIV infections attributed to heterosexual contact declined slightly in 2000, from 2,506 to 2,448. Female AIDS cases attributed to heterosexual contact declined from 4,281 to 3,981, down

AIDS Cases Are Declining

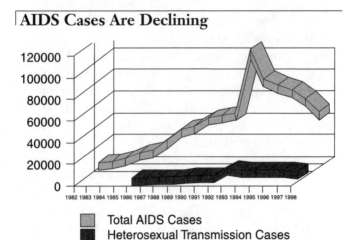

Centers for Disease Control and Prevention, *Amerian Outlook*, Spring 2000.

in turn from 6,253 in 1993. When a decline is the "most rapid" area of growth, how bad can things be?

Gayle also cited studies indicating that young homosexual males are showing a clear increase in risky behavior. Yet even this bad news is the inevitable result of good news—wisely or not, people are making risk-benefit decisions based on the availability of new therapies. While those drugs have not yet made full-blown AIDS a controllable condition like diabetes, it appears they have done so with HIV infection. Seen Magic Johnson lately? A decade after his diagnosis he's become a bit pudgy, but otherwise seems no worse for the wear.

Would-be risk-takers probably should think a bit harder about the tremendous costs and sometimes serious side effects of anti-HIV medicines. But they're apparently assuming that with new therapies coming out all the time, they probably will never get AIDS. And they're probably right. (For her dedication in providing such useful information for the past six years, Gayle has now been hired by the Bill and Melinda Gates Foundation to direct their AIDS funding activities.)

Minorities

You CAN find bad news in the CDC report. For example, every year minorities constitute a greater share of the AIDS reaper's victims. Blacks have about ten times the AIDS rate of whites, Hispanics four times. *The Myth of Heterosexual AIDS* [was] published in 1990. In a book that many stores and one giant chain resolutely refused to stock, I detailed the obsession with portraying the disease as one of heterosexual middle-class whites, and the deadly disinformation spread by politically-correct slogans such as "Everyone's at Risk" and "AIDS Is an Equal Opportunity Destroyer."

"To the extent (government and the media) failed to give minorities much-needed extra attention, they left them in the back of the bust—or the back of a hearse," I wrote.

I was right. But forgive me if I don't feel like gloating.

"[The AIDS] tragedy threatens to engulf the world if lifestyles do not change and researchers cannot come up with a cure."

The Global AIDS Epidemic Is a Serious Problem

Ian Murray

Ian Murray is a medical correspondent for the *London Times*. In the following viewpoint, Murray warns that the AIDS epidemic has entered its third phase, in which heterosexuals are now equally at risk of contracting HIV as homosexuals and injecting drug users. Due to the spread of HIV into the heterosexual population, the number of women with AIDS will soon surpass the number of men infected. The AIDS epidemic in Africa and Asia is severe, he asserts, and the tragedy of global AIDS will worsen unless a cure is found and people change their lifestyles.

As you read, consider the following questions:
1. What proportion of women were infected with HIV in 1998, according to Murray?
2. In the author's opinion, what factors are largely responsible for the spread of HIV in Africa?
3. Where are the lowest rates of HIV infection in the world, as cited by Murray?

If you read at an average speed, this article should take you five minutes to finish. By the time you reach the end, 50 people around the world will have died from AIDS and another 55 will have become infected with HIV. Inevitably, that means more people will be dying of the disease in a decade or so than are dying today. Virtually every country in the world has seen new infections over the past year, and in some places the epidemic is out of control.

The Third Wave

AIDS is now in what amounts to a third wave of infection; like the first, it is coming out of Africa. The first wave largely infected homosexual men. The second involved people who injected drugs. The third wave is among heterosexuals, which means that now virtually everyone who leads a normal sex life is at risk. The result is that women now appear to be heading for an unwelcome equality with men in terms of HIV infection on a worldwide level. In 1997, they accounted for 41 percent of infected adults. In 1998 the proportion grew to 43 percent of all those over 15 with disease.

It cannot be long, if present trends continue, before women become the majority. Since the start of the epidemic around 20 years ago, HIV has infected more than 47 million people, of whom nearly 14 million have died. More than 95 percent of those infected live in the developing world, and those who die are mostly young adults, who would be in their most productive period of life. Their loss has grave consequences for the poor countries that urgently need their drive and energy, depriving the economy of the very people needed to make it thrive, overburdening primitive health services, and creating tens of thousands of dependent orphans.

AIDS is thus undermining even the most determined efforts to build strong, self-reliant nations. Nowhere is this more evident than in South Africa, which trailed some of its neighbors in infection levels in the early part of the 1990s but is now catching up fast. The mines, which are the backbone of the nation's economy, are much to blame for this. Workers are attracted to the mines, not only from rural areas but from neighboring countries with low job opportunities and high HIV rates. They come from places like Zimbabwe—probably the epicenter of the epidemic—where around 1 in 10 of the population is infected and up to half the pregnant women carry the disease.

Carltonville, in the heart of the gold belt, has 88,000 miners, of whom 60 percent are migrant workers. Their relatively high wages attract prostitutes and drug peddlers. The result is that 22 percent of the miners are now infected, twice the national average, and the miners go home on leave and take the infection back with them. Civil war and revolution in sub-Saharan Africa have also helped to spread the disease rapidly.

In Rwanda, refugees from the towns, where infection rates are high, have carried the disease into the countryside, where infection rates were low. Refugee camps have been breeding grounds for the illness, and rates there are as much as six times higher than the 11 percent national average. Rape has also played its part. Infection rates among victims are 17 percent compared with 11 percent.

Outside Africa

Outside Africa, the growth rate is highest in Asia, with 7 million in the continent now infected. There are signs that it is beginning to spread in earnest through the vast, overcrowded populations of India and China. As in Africa, the infection is spread mostly by heterosexuals.

In India, AIDS was largely restricted to the towns, but recent studies have shown that it is spreading into the countryside, largely due to the promiscuous behaviour of long-distance truck drivers. The sex industry in countries such as Thailand and the Philippines is also playing a sinister and dangerous role. Young girls are sold by their poverty-stricken parents into the sex trade. They will almost inevitably catch the disease, then bring it back to their remote villages.

In most other areas of the world, IV drug use and homosexual sex are the main reasons for the disease's continued spread. The drug-injecting communities of eastern Europe and Central Asia—where the disease was little known until the mid 1990s—are now hotbeds of infection. Ukraine is the worst affected, with the Russian Federation, Belarus, and Moldova not far behind. Although there is little evidence yet that heterosexual carriers in this area are spreading the disease, the close links between drugs and sex make this almost inevitable in the near future.

Regional HIV/AIDS Statistics and Features, End of 2001

	Adults & children living with HIV/AIDS	Adults & children newly infected with HIV	Adult prevalence rate*	% of HIV-positive adults who are women
Sub-Saharan Africa	28.1 million	3.4 million	8.4%	55%
North Africa & Middle East	440,000	80,000	0.2%	40%
South and South-East Asia	6.1 million	800,000	0.6%	35%
East Asia & Pacific	1 million	270,000	0.1%	20%
Latin America	1.4 million	130,000	0.5%	30%
Caribbean	420,000	60,000	2.2%	50%
Eastern Europe & Central Asia	1 million	250,000	0.5%	20%
Western Europe	560,000	30,000	0.3%	25%
North America	340,000	45,000	0.6%	20%
Australia & New Zealand	15,000	500	0.1%	10%
TOTAL	40 million	5 million	1.2%	48%

*The proportion of adults (15 to 49 years of age) living with HIV/AIDS in 2001, using 2001 population numbers.

UNAIDS, December 1, 2001.

Western Europe, like North America, has been wealthy enough to check the death rate from AIDS by supplying victims with the new drug cocktails that control the disease and delay death. Because more people are becoming infected in these areas, largely through homosexual sex or drug injection, the proportion of the population with HIV is growing, adding to the problems of control. On the credit side, safe sex campaigns are having an impact, with around 60 percent of young people now using condoms and the proportion growing steadily every year.

In Latin America, the adult prevalence rate is so far relatively low, given the high populations, crowded conditions, and serious poverty. The sex industry in the cities is causing an inexorable increase in infection, however, while homosexual and drug-taking communities are among the least likely in the world to take precautions. Transmission of AIDS through sex between men and women is especially prominent in the Caribbean, with rates of 8 percent among pregnant women in Haiti and the Dominican Republic.

The lowest rates anywhere are in Australia and New Zealand, where only 0.1 percent of the population and 5 percent of pregnant women are infected with HIV. All round the world, however, there are 33.4 million now living what will be an inevitably shortened life with HIV. The number is huge, but each case is an individual tragedy. That tragedy threatens to engulf the world if lifestyles do not change and researchers cannot come up with a cure.

"*People are not dying of AIDS but of the diseases that have always afflicted those parts of the globe where the water is not clean and sewage is not properly disposed of.*"

The African AIDS Epidemic Is Exaggerated

Tom Bethell

American health organizations exaggerate the number of AIDS cases in Africa in an attempt to acquire more funding for research and other programs, contends Tom Bethell in the following viewpoint. He asserts that Africans diagnosed with AIDS are not tested for HIV. In addition, common tropical diseases have been reclassified as AIDS-defining illnesses in order to boost the number of AIDS cases in Africa. Millions of people are dying in Africa, but Bethell argues that they are not dying of AIDS. Bethell is the Washington correspondent for the monthly magazine *American Spectator*.

As you read, consider the following questions:

1. According to Bethell, what disease did the Centers for Disease Control add as AIDS-defining in order to increase the number of women with AIDS?
2. What are the major components of the definition of AIDS in Africa, as cited by the author?
3. What is the problem with the Bangui definition of AIDS, according to Charles Gilks?

Hype about AIDS in Africa has reached new heights. [Former] Secretary of State Madeleine Albright and [former] Vice President Al Gore (at the U.N. Security Council) have declared it to be an international security threat. AIDS is now called the leading cause of death in Africa, with over two million deaths in 1999, and the epidemic in sub-Saharan Africa is spreading "nearly unabated." Seventy percent of all AIDS cases are said to be African. On *Newsweek's* cover we read of "10 Million Orphans." Meanwhile, in a "Tour of Light," a troupe of orphans from "devastated Uganda" performs on the Kennedy Center stage. There are calls for a new Marshall Plan.

Skepticism Is Scarce

Skepticism about what governments say—always scarce among journalists—vanishes completely when it comes to "plagues" and epidemics. At the mention of AIDS, newspaper stories are virtually dictated by public health officials. The *New York Times* is the pre-eminent example, with other publications trotting behind uncritically. A rare exception is the science journalist Michael Fumento, now with the Hudson Institute. Another is Charles Geshekter, a professor of African history at California State University at Chico. He has made 15 trips to Africa and has written widely about AIDS in that continent.

The author of *The Myth of Heterosexual AIDS*, Fumento told me that he found the recent reports of HIV infection rates of 25 percent in some African countries to be not believable. The alarmist predictions about the progress of AIDS in this country have not been borne out, he said. African AIDS is an attempt to find the bad news elsewhere. Here, AIDS has not spread into the general population, and never will. It has remained confined to the major "risk groups," mainly intravenous drug users and fast-lane homosexuals. But in Africa, more women than men are said to be infected with the virus. Prof. Geshekter, too, sees African AIDS as a prolongation of the gravy train for public health experts. "AIDS is dwindling away in this country," he told me. "The numbers are down. What are the AIDS educators to do? Africa beckons."

An African AIDS Primer

Here is an "African AIDS" primer. Over the years AIDS American-style was redefined more and more expansively. In 1993, for example, the Centers for Disease Control (CDC) in Atlanta added cervical cancer to the list of AIDS-defining diseases, with the unacknowledged goal of increasing the numbers of women. The overwhelming preponderance of males was an embarrassment to infectious-disease epidemiology, given that the viral agent was supposed to be sexually transmitted. AIDS is a name for 30-odd diseases found in conjunction with a positive test for antibodies to the human immunodeficiency virus. Being "HIV positive," then, is the unifying requirement for an AIDS case. Here is the key point that the newspapers won't tell you. To diagnose AIDS in Africa, no HIV test is needed. The presence of the unifying agent that supposedly causes the immune deficiency, the ID of AIDS, does not have to be established.

This was decided by public health officials at an AIDS conference in Bangui, a city in the Central African Republic, in October 1985. This meeting was engineered by an official from the CDC, Joseph McCormick. He wanted to establish a diagnostic definition of AIDS to be used in poor countries that lacked the equipment to do blood tests. He also succeeded in persuading representatives from the World Health Organization (WHO) in Geneva to set up its own AIDS program. The appearance of sick people in Zaire hospitals had persuaded McCormick and others that AIDS now existed in Africa—this before HIV tests had even been conducted. And here was something important to write home about: Slightly more women than men were affected. Back in America, as Laurie Garrett wrote in *The Coming Plague* (1994), McCormick told an assistant secretary of Health and Human Services that "there's a one to one sex ratio of AIDS cases in Zaire." Heterosexual transmission had been established. Now we were all at risk! AIDS budgets would soar.

Redefining AIDS

The CDC had an "urgent need to begin to estimate the size of the AIDS problem in Africa," McCormick wrote in his book, *Level 4: Virus Hunters of the CDC.*

Only then could we figure out what needed to be done—and where. This is what is known as surveillance. It involves counting the number of cases of AIDS. But we had a peculiar problem with AIDS. Few AIDS cases in Africa receive any medical attention at all. No diagnostic tests, suited to widespread use, yet existed. . . . We needed a clinical case definition—that is to say, a set of guidelines a clinician could follow in order to decide whether a certain person had AIDS or not. This was my major goal: if I could get everyone at the WHO meeting in Bangui to agree on a single, simple definition of what an AIDS case was in Africa, then, imperfect as the definition might be, we could actually start to count the cases, and we would all be counting roughly the same thing.

His goal was achieved. The "Bangui definition," was reached "by consensus." It has proven useful, McCormick added, "in determining the extent of the AIDS pandemic in Africa, especially in areas where no testing is available." Here are the major components of the definition: "prolonged fevers (for a month or more), weight loss of 10 percent or greater, and prolonged diarrhea." No HIV test, of course. What this meant was that many traditional African diseases, pandemic in poverty-stricken areas with tropical climate, open latrines, and contaminated drinking water, could now be called something else: AIDS.

The Bangui redefinition was published in CDC's *Morbidity and Mortality Weekly Report*, and in *Science* magazine (November 21, 1986), but you would be hard put to find it in our major newspapers. Take the *New York Times*, whose main AIDS reporter has long been Lawrence K. Altman. He is himself a former public health officer, and like McCormick worked for the CDC's Epidemic Intelligence Service. He wrote the first newspaper article on AIDS, in 1981, and in November 1985 wrote two huge stories for the *Times* on African AIDS. "To this reporter," he wrote in the first, "who is also a physician and who has examined AIDS patients and interviewed dozens of doctors while traveling through Africa, the disease is clearly a more important public health problem than many African governments acknowledge." The story filled an entire inside page of the paper, and it included a "box" on the Bangui meeting. It mentioned a "hospital surveillance system to determine the extent of AIDS," but Dr. Altman omitted to say that, in

Africa, AIDS could now be diagnosed without an HIV test.

The obvious problem was pointed out by Charles Gilks in the *British Medical Journal* in 1991. Persistent diarrhea with weight loss can be associated with "ordinary enteric parasites and bacteria," as well as with opportunistic infection, he wrote. "In countries where the incidence of tuberculosis is high," as it is in Africa, "substantial numbers of people reported as having AIDS may in fact not have AIDS." By then, the *Times* had published another huge series on African AIDS, this one reported by Eric Eckholm and John Tierney. It emphasized the need for condom distribution in Africa ("since 1968, A.I.D. has given 7 billion condoms to developing countries") but the reporters again overlooked the relaxed definition.

Unlike dysentery and malaria, of course, plagues and epidemics reward reporters with front-page stories. And the

---

AIDS Is Not Killing Africans

The World Health Organization defines an AIDS case in Africa as a combination of fever, persistent cough, diarrhea and a 10 per cent loss of body weight in two months. No HIV test is needed. It is impossible to distinguish these common symptoms—all of which I've had while working in Somalia—from those of malaria, tuberculosis or the indigenous diseases of impoverished lands.

By contrast, in North America and Europe, AIDS is defined as 30-odd diseases in the presence of HIV (as shown by a positive HIV test). The lack of any requirement for such a test in Africa means that, in practice, many traditional African diseases can be and are reclassified as AIDS. Since 1994, tuberculosis itself has been considered an AIDS-indicator disease in Africa.

Dressed up as HIV/AIDS, a variety of old sicknesses have been reclassified. Post mortems are seldom performed in Africa to determine the actual cause of death. According to the Global Burden of Disease Study, Africa maintains the lowest levels of reliable vital statistics for any continent—a microscopic 1.1 per cent. "Verbal autopsies" are widely used because death certificates are rarely issued. When AIDS experts are asked to prove actual cases of AIDS, terrifying numbers dissolve into vague estimates of HIV infection.

Charles Geshekter, *Globe and Mail*, March 14, 2000.

---

budget requests of public health departments are met with alacrity. It was mutually convenient, surely, even if coincidental, that Altman and McCormick emerged from the same CDC intelligence service.

Sweeping Extrapolations

The loose definition has allowed health officials to conduct small surveys and make sweeping extrapolations to entire nations: AIDS is running rampant! Ten million orphans! (*Newsweek* might have told us that, in WHO lingo, an "orphan" is someone under 15 whose mother has died. With life expectancy short, and fertility rates high, it is to be expected that a lot of African children are still under 15 when their mother dies.)

In a forthcoming article, Michael Fumento comments on the vagueness of the Third World AIDS estimates, "made by organizations that are given more funds if they declare there's more AIDS." He adds:

> The Statistical Assessment Service [STATS] in Washington D.C. has noted recently that the World Health Organization in its latest ranking of the world's greatest killers dropped TB down the list while moving AIDS up. The best explanation, STATS director of research David Murray told me, is that WHO noted that many Third World AIDS victims also suffer from TB, that both AIDS and TB data are just educated guesses, and so felt justified in simply shifting a huge chunk of deaths out of the TB category into AIDS. He was unable to get anyone from the organization to comment.

That surely is what happened. The CDC added TB to its list of AIDS-defining diseases in 1993, and, with no need for an HIV test in Africa, TB falls under the "AIDS" umbrella. All along, incidentally, someone has been keeping a stricter tally of the AIDS cases actually reported to the WHO. The organization's *Weekly Epidemiological Record* (November 26, 1999) states that a cumulative total of 794,444 cases of AIDS in Africa has been reported to Geneva since 1982. "Anyone who wants to disprove those numbers should provide better, locally based figures," says Charles Geshekter of Cal State University. "So far, no one has."

In South Africa, which he visited recently, Geshekter found that HIV tests are conducted at prenatal clinics and the results extrapolated across the country. One problem is that pregnancy is only one of the many conditions that trigger a "false positive result." The reaction is not specific to HIV. Antibodies to many other endemic infections also trigger false HIV alarms. The problem has been well known for 15 years, and it alone renders all African AIDS projections meaningless.

Unclean Conditions

Yes, people are dying all over Africa. The continent's population, whether sub-Saharan or supra-, continues to climb rapidly all the same. People are not dying of AIDS but of the diseases that have always afflicted those parts of the globe where the water is not clean and sewage is not properly disposed of. Poverty, unclean water, and tropical weather make for insalubrious conditions. They have been exacerbated by civil war and the vast conflict raging in and around Central Africa. During his recent visit, Prof. Geshekter asked a woman from a rural Zulu township what made her neighbors sick. She mentioned tuberculosis and the open latrine pits next to village homes. "The flies, not sex, cause 'running tummy,'" she said. Her understanding of public health would seem to be more advanced than that of the highly paid health officers who fly in from Atlanta and Geneva.

A sub-Saharan male-and-female AIDS epidemic implies that Africans have abandoned themselves to reckless sexual promiscuity. Recreational drug use is not alleged, and it is well established that it takes a thousand sexual contacts on average to transmit HIV heterosexually. (That is why HIV has stayed confined to risk groups in the West.) Fables of insatiable African truck-drivers and rampant prostitution— Beverly Hills morals imputed to African villagers—are attempts to rationalize the equal-gender epidemiology of AIDS in Africa. Moslem countries to the north are less likely to accept this libel, so we may predict that the "epidemic" will remain firmly sub-Saharan. Cairo is a river's journey away from the Uganda hotbeds, and yet WHO reports a demure cumulative total of 215 cases in Egypt (pop. 65 million) since AIDS began.

> *"It is unfair and hurtful to speak of us as irresponsible and too illiterate to be able to understand how to use medicines and keep track of complicated regimens."*

Access to Cheap Drugs Can Slow the AIDS Epidemic in Africa

Chatinkha C. Nkhoma

Chatinkha C. Nkhoma is a single mother from Malawi, Africa, who is HIV-positive. The following viewpoint is from her written testimony to Congress on July 22, 1999. She argues that AIDS has devastated Africa. So many adults are dying that there is no one left to raise the children. Nkhoma asserts that prevention efforts have failed because they preach morality instead of protection. If AIDS medications are available to Africans, she contends that people will get themselves tested so that they can receive the drugs for treatment and thus slow the spread of the disease. The only way to save millions of Africans from dying of AIDS is to give Africa access to the life-saving drugs.

As you read, consider the following questions:
1. Who has died of AIDS among Nkhoma's family?
2. What is the only vaccine available for AIDS, in the author's opinion?
3. According to the author, how many Africans die every day of AIDS?

Chatinkha C. Nkhoma, congressional testimony, *US Role in Combating HIV/AIDS: Chatinkha C. Nkhoma*, Federal Document ClearingHouse Inc., July 22, 1999.

The first time I came to America was in 1991 after completing a one and half year study of the German language in Bonn, Germany. I came here to chase the Malawian woman's dream combined with the American dream. That is to get a higher education and gain financial independence and security. I proceeded to enroll at Montgomery College, paying for my tuition doing odd manual jobs. I completed the first semester as an A student. I applied and received a scholarship from my government, which enabled me to enter a four-year college at George Washington University in the Fall of 1992. After my graduation with a BA in International Affairs from the George Washington University in 1995, I headed straight back to Malawi, Africa with overflowing enthusiasm and full of anticipation of the good times to come. I was assigned to the Foreign Affairs ministry and rose fast from being a regional desk officer to the post of deputy director.

As a woman in a male-dominated community, this was not an easy feat. I had to overcome many barriers and obstacles, traditional, socioeconomic and gender, which affected my life both positively and negatively. I achieved success the hard way, not having to pay with sexual favors (a common trend in my country). Thus I did not gain popularity, but respect.

I was on my path, I was aspiring to become an Ambassador for my country and whatever the future held for me, maybe United Nations (UN) Secretary General. All these dreams had a time frame. But my world came tumbling down when I experienced a near-death battle with PCP pneumonia resulting in being diagnosed with AIDS. No, this news did not come as a surprise to me, even after the fact that I had tried my best to avoid infection by doing the right things. It did not come as a surprise because AIDS and death were now fully integrated in the everyday life of my surroundings. AIDS had been circulating around me and was drawing closer. I had bargained with God every day to spare me, I promised him I would be good. But as members of my own family began to die, the trap felt tighter. I knew my turn was near. And as sure as the sun will shine, it came, and with it my dreams died.

Other Plans

They died, but God had other plans for me. I got a little better and traveled to America to pursue a Masters degree study. It was then that I discovered that I wouldn't have to die as soon as I had thought. There were these new drugs which, I learnt, would allow me to live longer. The advances in the treatment of AIDS had gone beyond only AZT. These treatments, that meant that nobody needed to have to die right away. It meant that hope would be restored for people dying from AIDS. Since that discovery, I have been unable to think of anything else except to see that these new wonder drugs are available for poor people dying with AIDS. Unfortunately, the cost of these drugs turned my dream into a nightmare.

Now however, my dream is still to become an ambassador, but a different type of ambassador. Advocate for the voiceless million who desperately need these drugs. I am here to represent the crying Mother Africa, her children have suffered long enough. History is my witness. Every time I take these drugs, I cannot help but feel guilty, knowing that my brothers, sisters, mothers, fathers, daughters, sons, uncles, aunts, our children, tomorrow's leaders and they are all dying, slowly and painfully because they are too poor to afford them. It is now not about my survival, but the survival of millions of people sentenced to death and their only crime is that of being poor. A friend here once asked me what I was going to do if I went back home without these drugs. I told her make the question 'What I would want on my tombstone'?

Every Mother's Nightmare

Every day messages from home are of someone I know, dying of AIDS-related illness. My neighbors, work colleagues, friends, local entertainers, politicians, many members of the cabinet and parliament are dying. Everybody is dying. Personally, I have lost my brother Mike, my sister Eleanor, three brother-in-laws, cousins, aunts and uncles, all dying in the span of less than 6 years. This is too much for my mother. She has now developed high blood pressure problem, something that we have never had in our family history.

She laments that she never imagined she would be burying her children, but her children and grandchildren burying her. A woman with very minimal education (grade 3), raised 9 of her own children and 7 from other relations on her own as a farmer (my father died in 1978), to levels of college. It was now her time to be enjoying the fruits of her labor. But no, at the age of 72 she is busy caring for her sick and dying children. This breaks my heart more than my infection. Her survival depends on us, she is too old to continue with this. I have to go back and look after her, but I cannot without the medication. Please help me to go back and spend my last years, not days, with my son and family. It hurts too much thinking about what my child's future would be like without me, it is every mother's nightmare.

Pett. © 1997 by *Lexington Herald-Leader*. Reprinted with permission.

Please allow us to have access to the treatment drug so we can raise our children a little longer and not leave them as orphans. This is the cry of every poor mother infected with the disease. If you can save the newborn, you must save the mother, because it is only the mother that gives total commitment to the healthy development of her baby (even if that baby is 60 years old). Orphanages can only do so much.

Traditionally, when a mother dies, her children are raised by her relatives, but the intensity of which the AIDS epidemic has increased deaths of mothers combined with the frail economies, makes this practice difficult to maintain. . . .

Lives Can Be Saved

It is unfair and hurtful to speak of us as irresponsible and too illiterate to be able to understand how to use medicines and keep track of complicated regimens. We who have never had these drugs are not the cause of multidrug-resistant HIV yet. To say we should be condemned to death is practicing politics of genocide. There are even those who say our health care workers are not smart enough. They are smart enough to know that there is no point for them to learn the intricacies of combinatorial antiviral therapy when there are no drugs to use and when they are overworked trying to make the dying suffer less. We have learnt your languages, technologies and even your culture. Is it really possible that we would be unable to learn how to take medication that can save our lives? I don't think so.

A recent television news item argued that it was better to allow Africans to die for fear of resistant strains of virus. May I point out that there is never a valid humane argument which allows for the death of over 40 million people, it should not be allowed. It is our human responsibilities to save each other and not allow unnecessary deaths. We should be here talking about how to save these poor people, not arguing on why it should be done. If lives can be saved, it is humanity to do so, regardless of the costs. In my country we say, money does not make people, but people make people. People are people because there are other people. The differences in shades of our skins are there because they are there. It is neither a bad or good thing, it is just there, not to prove anything at all and should not be used to value the worth of one's life.

Prevention Has Failed

Prevention campaign efforts have so far proved to be a failure, because they targeted morality more than mortality. Emphasis is more on the 'wages of sin' syndrome so people naturally prefer to hide their positive status or not get tested at all. This leads to continual unchecked spread of the virus. It also triggers discriminations. Prevention messages have negatively portrayed women as the major culprit. Women are victimized, some by having all the family property taken away by a deceased husband's relatives and leaving her and her children homeless.

With drugs available as part of the prevention programs, more people will want to get tested so that they are put on medication. Discrimination of those of us infected will reduce. When we are receiving care we will feel more obliged to control further spreading of the virus and help in outreach peer-education to rest of the populations. On the other hand, condemning us to death is not helping the situation. Those condemned cannot feel any obligation to get involved in the fight against this deadly virus, both knowingly and unknowingly. So it is very important that care for those infected is included with any assistance offered with foreign aid programs to effectively control this tragic epidemic. Only together and when greed is removed, can we succeed in eventually combating this virus.

I know how hard people here try to stay alive and be compliant, that is why the infection rate has since reduced to 50% with treatment of these new drugs. This can also happen with us, because, I can assure you of one thing, where there is a will there is a way. Condemning millions of people because of unfounded fears is not the answer. There is no proof that we will not be able to adhere to drug requirements. We have adhered to many complex treatment regimens that have since successfully eradicated or brought under control chronic diseases. These prophets of doom are only driven by greed, blind murderous greed. There is no factual evidence to their claim and it is better to try and fail any rescue efforts than never to try at all. The will for a human being to live supersedes science. Let us not underestimate this fact. Africans can walk over a 10 mile distance every day to get a treatment if that is a requirement. It is no secret that we are in need of many other things. But that is not a valid reason to allow millions of people to die because they are poor.

Give Africans Life-Saving Drugs

I want to go home. But to go home is to go to my suffering death. And to stay here and be silent is to suffer inside knowing how many millions of my people are sick with an illness your government has found ways to treat. Let Africa have rights and tools to try and save its people. Allow us access to these life-saving drugs. This is the only way we can be able to survive. That is not asking for too much. It is not fair to punish Africa without a crime. That is what is happening now.

We all know that Africans have contributed in the AIDS research. Some people lost their lives being used as guinea pigs researching the current AIDS treatments. Countries such as Uganda, Kenya, Tanzania, Zimbabwe, Zambia and Malawi have AIDS research projects still underway being run by U.S.A. institutions such as Johns Hopkins. It seems like these AIDS research projects are not meant for Africans' benefit. Why else would it be such a big deal to allow us to use them?

Over 13 million Africans have already died, over 20 million are dying and over 20 percent will be joining the category every year without these life-saving medicines, for in matters of life and death everyone must have a right to their share of the necessities of life. These medicines are necessities for life for those of us who are HIV-positive.

Lives Before Profits

A program which tests and treats will also stop the virus from spreading any further and this is the only vaccine available. It works, and we need to use it now. If we do not come together then we will be watching the greatest killing of any event in history unfold, at the same time we know exactly how to stop it. This would be unforgivable. Do not let it be said that the only thing that told the difference between those who would live and those who would die during the days of the great plague was the color of a person's skin. Let us put lives before profits, it can be done and must be done.

Every day that we waste in arguing over who should live and should die, according to the United Nations Secretary General, 5,000 more Africans die of AIDS. This human carnage can be stopped. We need to stop this insanity.

In the end, it cannot be in the interests of your companies to be responsible, along with your government, for the deaths of millions of people, and that is what the world will come to decide if this war against poor countries continues. When the drugs are available, we the children of Africa wherever we are, in America, Caribbean, Europe, Asia and Africa, will celebrate by singing and playing our drums and horns so loud you will hear us in this house. Mother Africa will begin to wipe away her tears, smiling, because Mother Earth will be waking up to stop her children from hurting everywhere. She will wake up and stop the CHAOS. Let the last couple of months of this horrible millennium be a positive beginning of the next millennium.

This is the cry of the voiceless. The dying millions.

"If they were to give away the drugs to combat HIV, AIDS would continue to kill millions in Africa."

Prevention, Not Cheap Drugs, Can Eradicate AIDS in Africa

Robert Baker

Robert Baker is a specialist registrar in infectious diseases and HIV in a teaching hospital in London. In the following viewpoint, he argues that supplying anti-AIDS drugs to Africa would not reduce the spread of AIDS and might even increase it. To fight AIDS, a combination of at least three drugs must be taken, and the drugs must be taken according to a strict regimen. If they are not, the AIDS virus quickly becomes resistant to the drugs. Baker maintains that it would be nearly impossible for infected Africans to take the drugs correctly, which would then lead to a resistant strain of HIV. The best course for Africa, Baker contends, is to practice prevention and work on developing a vaccine for AIDS.

As you read, consider the following questions:
1. What is responsible for the spread of AIDS in Africa, according to Baker?
2. How does the cure rate for tuberculosis in the Third World compare to the cure rate in Britain, according to the author?
3. In the author's opinion, what should the banners of protesters outside drug companies be saying?

The South African President, Thabo Mbeki, is right to say that HIV is not responsible for the spread of AIDS in Africa. Poverty is. The pharmaceutical companies are regularly condemned for being unscrupulous and money-grubbing, but the fact is that if they were to give away the drugs to combat HIV, AIDS would continue to kill millions in Africa. Indeed, if the drugs were free, the death toll might rise.

AIDS and HIV

This is not to suggest that Mr Mbeki has got his science right. You cannot contract AIDS without infection from HIV. There is really no doubt at all that it is the agent which so catastrophically destroys the immune systems of infected individuals. There are a few scientists, chief among them the American Alan Duesberg, who say that it does not, and they are wrong. No serious doctor or scientist could have witnessed the remarkable improvement in the health of HIV-infected individuals on modern treatment without acknowledging that truth. The mortality from AIDS in some British hospitals has fallen tenfold since the drugs became available. The drugs work—which is just as well, given their cost.

To begin with they did not work. Initially, each promising drug was met with rapid disappointment as the virus became resistant. And then, in 1995, the penny dropped—some might say a bit belatedly. What was needed was not single drugs, but a combination of at least three.

New drugs have come—and gone—but that is the essence of treatment. With these drugs you can prevent HIV from developing into full-blown AIDS and even bring the desperately ill back from the brink. Sadly, though, it is not that simple. If you do not take the drugs properly, the virus comes back in a resistant form which may be impossible to treat. 'Properly' means that you really need adherence approaching 100 per cent to the drug regimen. Treatment—as far as we know—needs to be maintained for a lifetime, because the virus simply comes back if it is stopped.

In Britain HIV units have achieved the best results in the world. Encouraging 100 per cent adherence is a tremendous feat achieved by dedicated and inspired teams of nurses, doctors, health advisers, community specialists, scientists and pharmacists. Patients attend regularly for follow-up in clinics and have a battery of expensive tests performed at every attendance. All drugs have side-effects and these need to be screened for (a major cause of HIV morbidity and mortality is now drug complications), and you have to test for response of, and resistance to, the virus.

Drugs Will Not Cure AIDS in Africa

It is absurd to suppose that Western medicine will solve the problem in Africa. Even if the drugs were provided free, you would need, by African standards, impossibly expensive support facilities to monitor the effects of treatment. One major London teaching hospital has a budget of about 20 million [pounds sterling] a year to treat 2,000 patients with HIV. This compares with a per capita healthcare budget for all medical problems of $20 per person per year in Uganda, which is far from the poorest of African nations.

More than a Medical Problem

While AIDS experts agree that the steep price cuts enacted by some of the world's largest pharmaceutical companies were an important and welcome step, they say the move will have a limited effect in Africa until a host of other issues are dealt with. These include combating the grinding poverty that makes almost any charge unaffordable, creating a health care infrastructure to deliver the drugs and monitor their use, and educating people about AIDS.

"AIDS here is not a medical issue," said Marc Aguirre, a doctor with Hope Worldwide who runs an AIDS clinic in Abidjan that deals with some of the country's poorest HIV/AIDS patients. "It is a developmental problem, linked to social and economic conditions. It is a poverty issue."

Douglas Farah, *Washington Post*, June 12, 2001.

And that is where the problem lies. Without proper scientific support, just handing out free drugs in Africa will not cure people of HIV. This is my point and, for different reasons, Mbeki's. In Africa, AIDS is not a consequence of HIV but of poverty.

There is worse. Resistant virus can be transmitted from person to person, and by handing out drugs without proper back-up we would run the risk of a second wave of primarily resistant virus spreading worldwide. This is where the lesson from tuberculosis (TB) is vital. TB is a far easier disease to treat. In Britain we expect cure rates of greater than 90 per cent for the lung form, after usually just six months of treatment. Let us compare that with the situation in, for example, Nigeria. In one study it was established that nearly half of all drugs offered for treatment of TB there were out-of-date, incorrectly prescribed or fake.

Apart from money, you also need a social structure in which to implement your treatment. In a depressingly common development, the Nigerian study had to be abandoned halfway through because of civil unrest. The cure rate for TB in the Third World is, not surprisingly, about 10 per cent. Up to 15 per cent of isolates of TB in those countries show evidence of resistance, and there have already been outbreaks of fatal, multiply-resistant TB in London and New York.

What Can Be Done?

So what can be done in Africa? The answer is, to most HIV clinicians, screamingly obvious. There are already some limited measures in practice: routine condom use and public-health messages; treatment of sexually transmitted diseases which enhance HIV transmission; use of cheap, life-saving pneumonia preventers like Septrin; and Caesarean sections for affected mothers.

But what the banners of protesters outside the drug companies ought to be saying is not 'Free Drugs' but 'Where Are Your Vaccines?'. Most vaccines require one or two injections, in contrast to a lifetime's dependence on drugs that are proving highly lucrative, for the pharmaceutical industry. The number of scientists working on HIV vaccines throughout the world is about 100. Almost none of them works for commercial drug companies. As they say in America, go figure.

> *"We are watching [Africans with AIDS]*
> *die every day because the medicines they*
> *need are either too expensive or simply do*
> *not exist."*

Wealthy Countries Should Help Developing Countries Acquire AIDS Drugs

Rachel Cohen

While AIDS drugs are making a difference in the lives of patients in wealthy nations, millions of people in developing countries are dying because the drugs are too expensive for them. In the following viewpoint, Rachel Cohen asserts that the only alternative to treatment—prevention—has proved to be ineffective at controlling the disease in Africa. Forcing pharmaceutical companies to provide African countries with AIDS drugs at low cost is not a long-term, sustainable solution to the AIDS crisis, Cohen maintains. Rather, she contends that wealthy nations should provide funding to help developing countries acquire low-cost AIDS drugs. Cohen is an advocacy liaison for Médecins Sans Frontières's (Doctors Without Borders).

As you read, consider the following questions:

1. How many antiretroviral treatment programs does Médecins Sans Frontières (MSF) administer, according to the author?
2. What strategies does MSF recommend to ensure equitable access to affordable medicine?

Doctors Without Borders/Médecins Sans Frontières (MSF) is an international independent medical humanitarian organization. We run some 400 medical aid projects in over 85 countries. I hope to offer today the perspective of MSF field volunteers working to fight AIDS and other communicable diseases in poor countries throughout the world.

Not Just Numbers

The global AIDS crisis is finally making headlines in the United States. Public outcry over alarming death rates from the disease has at last begun to catalyze political action. For MSF, the recent attention paid to the AIDS pandemic and, to a lesser degree, other major communicable diseases such as malaria and tuberculosis, is welcome. But for us, the startling statistics—36 million people infected with HIV, 2 million deaths per year from TB, 300–500 million new cases of malaria each year—are not just numbers on a fact sheet or report. They are our patients, and we are watching them die every day because the medicines they need are either too expensive or simply do not exist.

Several weeks ago, a colleague from Nairobi, Kenya, Dr. Chris Ouma, visited the US as part of MSF's delegation to the United Nations General Assembly Special Session (UNGASS) on HIV/AIDS. He recounted one evening a chilling but all too common story about one of his patients, Simon. Simon had traveled to Nairobi from a neighboring village to see Dr. Ouma, and complained during the examination of severe headaches. No matter how many aspirins he took, the pain would not subside. Dr. Ouma ran a few tests and within minutes had confirmed the diagnosis he feared: cryptococcal meningitis, an HIV-related fungal infection that affects about one in every 10 people with AIDS and, if left untreated, is fatal, often within weeks. When Dr. Ouma returned to the examining room, he had to deliver not one, but two devastating blows: First, he had to tell Simon that he was HIV-positive. Second, he had to explain that, although an effective treatment existed, he could not prescribe it, because at $10 per pill, Simon would use his entire salary in just two weeks (and treatment with fluconazole, the effective drug, is for life). Although the same drug is available generically in Thailand for 10 cents a pill, Dr. Ouma had to explain to Simon, his wife, and their two children, that they should return home at once: Transporting a living body from Nairobi would be significantly less expensive than transporting a corpse. This is just one story among hundreds that MSF doctors in the field face on a daily basis.

MSF's field experience with the HIV/AIDS crisis began in the late 1980s. Initially, the organization devoted its resources to preventing the spread of the disease. By 1997, MSF was running 30 HIV/AIDS projects, still aimed primarily at prevention. However, by this time, powerful but expensive new drug "cocktails" of antiretroviral therapies were dramatically extending and improving the lives of people with AIDS in wealthy countries.

Meanwhile, infection rates soared in the developing world. It was clear that "prevention only" measures were not stemming the spread of the disease. In addition, for MSF doctors, it was unethical and unacceptable to send their patients home to die simply because the new medicines were unaffordable. With this in mind, the question was no longer whether to begin HIV/AIDS treatment in poor countries, but how.

Treatment Is Feasible

Although somewhat limited, MSF's field experience with HIV/AIDS shows what many already knew to be true: that offering treatment is indeed feasible, even in resource-limited settings. Although quantitative data from our projects are limited, my colleagues working in MSF's pilot antiretroviral treatment programs—there are currently nine such programs in seven countries—have found that offering the possibility of treatment is a powerful incentive for individuals to get tested and learn their HIV status, a crucial first step for effective prevention activities. In addition, they have found that the hope of treatment helps break the vicious cycle of denial of the disease and of social stigma associated with HIV. Offering treatment also motivates poor communities to mobilize resources and strengthen their health-care infrastructures.

Although more political attention than ever is focused on

the AIDS crisis in the developing world, challenges to adequate care and treatment for people living with HIV in resource-limited settings remain daunting. There is still an urgent need for operational research to determine how to best provide and monitor antiretroviral treatment in resource-poor settings. Substantial investment is also needed in healthcare delivery systems—personnel, diagnostics, supplies, equipment, and facilities—to sustain care for the long-term: Although the challenge of weak health systems in some areas is formidable, health infrastructure in developing countries is not homogeneous, and this challenge can no longer be used as an excuse to deny or delay increased access to life-prolonging medicines. But a reliable supply of antiretrovirals and other medically essential medicines with guaranteed long-term affordability is the first crucial step that must be taken in order

The Cost Gap of Fighting AIDS

At today's market prices, treating AIDS patients with antiretroviral medicines would cost more than the health care budgets of many developing countries. For some, including Uganda and Zimbabwe, the cost would dwarf the size of their national economies.

	Switzerland	Ivory Coast	Uganda	Zimbabwe
Population	7 million	14 million	21 million	12 million
People with HIV	12,000	700,000	930,000	3.5 million
Potential cost if all infected people were to be treated with antiretroviral drugs*	$144 million	8.4 billion	11.2 billion	18 billion
	*Three-drug combination therapy, at a mean cost of $12,000 a year			
Potential treatment cost as percent of Gross National Product	0.06%	84%	272%	265%
Average total health care spending, 1996–98, as percentage of GNP	7.1%	1.4%	1.8%	3.1%

Washington Post, December 28, 2000.

to ensure successful treatment (although not the only one).

Price is not the only reason that people with HIV/AIDS are not getting the medicines they need, but it remains a major barrier, and, as was agreed by all member states during UNGASS in New York in 2001, it must be addressed and overcome at all levels.

Financial Assistance Is a Priority

Increased financial resources from wealthy countries, including the US, is an urgent priority in the fight against AIDS and other diseases. In order to ensure that international funding mechanisms, including the proposed Global AIDS and Health Fund, can offer treatment to the highest number of people with HIV/AIDS, malaria, and TB, it is essential that funds be available for the purchase of medicines and medical technologies at the lowest possible cost. With that aim, MSF recommends the following mutually supportive strategies to ensure equitable and sustainable access to affordable medicines and related technologies:

- Stimulating generic competition, encouraging a differential (or tiered) pricing system, and creating economies of scale through regional or global procurement;
- Encouraging local production through voluntary licensing and technology transfer in countries with domestic drug manufacturing capacity; . . .
- Encouraging the purchase of medicines from lowest cost suppliers, including generic companies, to maximize the use of the available financial resources (intellectual property barriers need to be overcome by using legal exemptions to patent rights);
- Implementing health exceptions to patent rights for goods purchased with financing from internationally organized global funds;
- Creating a database of information on drug prices, quality, and patent status to help guide decisions of country purchasers.

It is critical that a long-term, sustainable solution to the crisis of lack of access to medicines be developed—not one that relies solely on the good will of pharmaceutical companies to voluntarily offer discounts on certain medicines.

Though such price reductions are important, they are extremely vulnerable strategies on their own.

MSF is painfully aware that our organization alone will not be able to provide treatment to all of those in need in the countries where we work. Today, our colleagues working in MSF programs in Malawi or Kenya or South Africa have to choose who will get treatment, and that means they have to choose who will live and who will die. This is an unacceptable position to be in as a physician. But imagine that you are the patient and you know that you will die not because effective treatments do not exist, but because the world has decided that it is too complex, not feasible, or not "cost-effective" to provide you with life-prolonging treatment.

Medical Treatment Should Be Provided

I'd like to close with a quotation from an MSF doctor working in Cameroon, Dr. Laura Ciaffi:

> Are the drugs everything? Of course not. Are AIDS patients still dying? Of course—by the thousands. But the availability of drugs is having an impact far beyond the relatively few people who are actually receiving them. We have to continue to insist on the principle that medical treatment for AIDS should be provided, even when we cannot do it for everyone and we cannot do it for everyone tomorrow. The principle makes all the difference. Five years ago, when I was an AIDS doctor in Italy, the first really effective antiretroviral combinations were becoming available in Europe. I recently went back to visit my old clinic in Milan, and I was so happy—but surprised—to meet many of my old patients. They were supposed to have died of AIDS years ago. One day, perhaps five years from now, I hope to come back to Cameroon to see the same thing.

"Physicians . . . want lower drug prices. They also want, and desperately need, infrastructure that will allow these drugs to be responsibly and effectively used [in Africa]."

Africa Needs Better Infrastructure, Not Drugs, to Fight AIDS

José M. Zuniga

José M. Zuniga is the president of the International Association of Physicians in AIDS Care. In the following viewpoint, Zuniga argues that donations of drugs by pharmaceutical companies are not enough to control the AIDS pandemic in Africa. Other elements necessary to transform AIDS from a fatal disease to a manageable one include adequate medical training, education, and facilities to diagnose, treat, and monitor AIDS; access to vaccines; and the political leadership to ensure that the proper steps are taken in the fight against AIDS. Without these important infrastructures, AIDS drugs will not be used effectively in the African pandemic.

As you read, consider the following questions:

1. Why does antiretroviral drug therapy require close monitoring by trained medical professionals, in the author's opinion?
2. What else should drug companies do to help control the spread of AIDS, in Zuniga's view?

S everal pharmaceutical companies announced plans in June 2000 to slash prices for their AIDS drugs as a mechanism to expand access to HIV/AIDS care in Africa. The importance of this declaration becomes even more apparent in the wake of figures from UNAIDS [joint United Nations Programme on HIV/AIDS], which estimates that 3 million people died from AIDS in the year 2000, and that approximately 36.1 million people are now HIV-infected worldwide.

In a world where the vast majority of people living with HIV/AIDS cannot obtain the level of HIV care that has proved clinically beneficial, the International Association of Physicians in AIDS Care (IAPAC) strongly encourages research-based drug manufacturers and others to facilitate greater access to medicines through lower-priced drug donations. In particular, drugs that reduce the risk of mother-to-child transmission should be made available. However, while drug donations are a key component of a comprehensive remedy, they alone will not make an appreciable dent in this pandemic.

As an African health official recently told me, "The companies can give us a supertanker of free products. Unfortunately, the drugs will only reach a small number of people with access to the medical knowledge and healthcare infrastructure that will allow them to be used correctly and, thus, improve their health." The other required elements in a comprehensive remedy for HIV/AIDS are infrastructure development, training and education, access to vaccines and microbicides, and political leadership.

More Is Needed

Strong medical and social infrastructure is necessary to support and sustain both ongoing basic healthcare and the introduction of antiretroviral drug combinations that can transform HIV from a certain death sentence into a manageable disease. Most Americans and Europeans do not realize that developing nations have severely constrained medical systems. Fundamental services taken for granted in other parts of the world are unavailable to the majority of African populations.

Physicians, where present, are often not trained in the basics of HIV diagnosis and treatment. A physician's knowledge has a positive impact on patients' treatment outcomes, quality of life and odds of surviving. In our push for solutions, IAPAC is developing an HIV medical training and certification program to accelerate physician training in resource-limited countries. This approach will quickly expand the cadre of local experts with the skills required for this highly specialized area of medical treatment, thus promoting the safe, optimal use of antiretroviral drugs.

Giveaways Are a Bad Idea

Giveaways sound good. Huge pharmaceutical companies make billions each year in profits. So why not force them to help the poor, who will otherwise die?

Because, in the end, giveaways are a bad idea. While drugs are an answer to the AIDS plague in North America and Western Europe, they are not the solution for Africa and many other extremely poor nations.

The reasons are simple. Drugs designed for people in more developed countries will not work as well for people living in countries that have no hospitals, clinics, clean water, sewers, roads or doctors. Some of these drugs must be taken with food to work effectively, for example. So in nations on the edge of famine, they will not do much good.

Arthur Caplan, www.msnbc.com, cited February 25, 2002.

Antiretroviral drug therapy requires close monitoring by trained medical professionals. Otherwise, these drugs are potentially dangerous to individuals and to the population at large. Because the HIV virus constantly replicates, or makes copies, it can adjust its DNA to "resist" obstacles such as antiretroviral drugs. This phenomenon, known as "drug resistance," presents a significant public health threat when medications are inappropriately prescribed or drug regimens are not properly followed. The threat of a mutant virus that resists known medications concerns many and cannot be underestimated or ignored. To this end, we strongly believe that drug companies and other entities must expand their largesse to include funding to educate people and to build health services to administer and monitor the use of these drugs.

Infrastructure development is not only important for improving access to life-saving medicines, but also for the deployment of vaccines and microbicides as they become available. Prevention measures such as vaccine and microbicide development and distribution are essential components of any comprehensive response to curb the spread of HIV/AIDS.

Political Leadership

Finally, political leadership is critical in addressing this issue. Individual countries need to acknowledge the problem and take positive action. Economic choices must be made responsibly. If we look at budget outlays in wealthier African countries, there is a disparity between what is spent on military defense versus what is allocated for basic healthcare, never mind care for HIV disease and its associated complications. What level of investment will be made to fight the virus? Which "enemy" poses the greater threat?

An effective remedy to this pandemic must combine education for clinicians, healthcare workers and the general population with an unwavering commitment from the leadership of the countries most affected by this virus. Moreover, this remedy must include a true commitment on all levels—public and private—to forge partnerships heretofore only dreamt about by policy wonks and idealists. Only then will the multitude of Africans living with and affected by HIV/AIDS receive the help they so desperately need.

Our members—10,000 physicians and healthcare professionals in 52 countries—want lower drug prices. They also want, and desperately need, infrastructure that will allow these drugs to be responsibly and effectively used. This approach, combined with support from the leadership of the countries themselves, will better the quality of care provided to all Africans living with HIV/AIDS.

Periodical Bibliography

The following articles have been selected to supplement the diverse views presented in this chapter.

Nell Boyce — "AIDS Is Far from Over," *U.S. News & World Report*, February 19, 2001.

Business Week — "How to Get AIDS Drugs to Africa," April 23, 2001.

John Cloud — "AIDS at 20," *Time*, June 11, 2001.

Michael Fumento — "AIDS: Making the Worst Out of a Good Situation," *American Outlook*, Spring 2000.

Bob Herbert — "Refusing to Save Africans," *New York Times*, June 11, 2001.

Doug Ireland — "AIDS Drugs for Africa," *Nation*, October 4, 1999.

Akin Jimoh — "Raise the Alarm Loudly: Africa Confronts the AIDS Pandemic," *Dollars and Sense*, May 2001.

Claudia Kalb — "We Have to Save Our People," *Newsweek*, July 24, 2000.

David Kirby — "AIDS: Could the Worst Be Yet to Come?" *Advocate*, February 1999.

Michael D. Lemonic — "Little Hope, Less Help," *Time*, July 24, 2000.

Johanna McGeary — "Death Stalks a Continent," *Time*, February 12, 2001.

Siddhartha Mukherjee — "Why Cheap Drugs for Africa Might Be Dangerous," *New Republic*, July 24, 2000.

Joshua Cooper Ramo — "The Real Price of Fighting AIDS," *Time*, July 9, 2001.

Lori Robinson — "After 20 Years, HIV/AIDS Disproportionately Threatens Black Populations Around the World," *Crisis*, May 2001.

Andrew Sullivan — "Profit of Doom?" *New Republic*, March 26, 2001.

Rachel L. Swarns — "A Bold Move on AIDS in South Africa," *New York Times*, February 5, 2002.

Robert Weissman — "AIDS Drugs for Africa," *Multinational Monitor*, September 1999.

Robert Weissman and Naomi Lopez — "Symposium: Are U.S. Anti-AIDS Drug Makers Being Unfair to Africa?" *Insight*, September 13, 1999.

CHAPTER 2

What Policies Should Be Adopted for HIV Testing?

Chapter Preface

Pregnant women who are HIV-positive can pass the infection on to their children during pregnancy, childbirth, and nursing. For several years, many states tested newborns for HIV, but because the results were confidential and for statistical purposes only, the mothers were not informed if their babies tested HIV-positive. Even if a baby is tested HIV-positive, however, that doesn't mean that he or she is infected. In fact, most babies—75 percent—who test positive for HIV are not really infected—their mother's antibodies are simply showing up in the test. However, if mothers are not informed that their babies tested positive, they remain ignorant of the fact that they themselves are infected. As a result, mothers may breast feed their babies without realizing that they could be passing on the infection. If steps are taken to prevent the transmission of infection from mother to baby, however, the mother's antibodies will pass from the baby's system in about a year, and the baby will not develop AIDS.

Nettie Mayersohn, a New York assemblywoman, fought for three years to pass a bill that required mandatory testing of pregnant women and that also required New York health officials to tell women if their babies test positive for HIV. She and her supporters argue that mandatory testing and notification allow both the mother and her baby to get treatment that can reduce the risk of HIV transmission before, during, and after childbirth. Without the treatment, she asserts, thousands of babies in New York were seroconverting to HIV-positive and dying from infections that could have been prevented.

Many people and organizations opposed Mayersohn's mandatory testing law, however. The American Civil Liberties Union maintains that mandatory testing is an invasion of the mother's right to privacy. In addition, the stigma and discrimination associated with HIV/AIDS is so severe that many women would forgo medical care in order to avoid testing. The ACLU asserts that all testing should be voluntary and the results confidential.

Testing for AIDS is a politically charged issue that pits an individual's right to privacy against public health safety. The authors in the following chapter debate several aspects of HIV testing, including whether the names of those who test positive should be reported to the government, whether the tests should be mandatory or voluntary, and whether former sexual partners should be notified about the results.

"[Few] respondents in . . . risk groups . . . indicated that [reporting their names to the government] was their main concern [for delaying the HIV test]."

States Should Be Required to Report the Names of People with HIV

Centers for Disease Control and Prevention

When the HIV/AIDS epidemic started in 1981, all cases of AIDS were reported to the Centers for Disease Control and Prevention (CDC), the nation's primary agency for protecting Americans' health, so that the spread of the disease could be tracked. In the following viewpoint, the CDC asserts that due to the success of antiviral drugs, the number of reported AIDS cases has dropped dramatically, yet the number of HIV infections is rising. Therefore, the CDC urges all states to report positive HIV test results so that the agency can continue to monitor the spread of the disease. The CDC reviewed data from numerous studies and found that reporting the names of those who tested HIV positive did not significantly deter people from taking the HIV test. The most common reason given for delaying or not taking an HIV test, the CDC maintains, is fear of the results, not name reporting.

As you read, consider the following questions:
1. According to the CDC, how does the percentage of HIV infections in adolescents and young adults compare to the percentage of AIDS cases in the same group?
2. What is the difference between confidential testing and anonymous testing, according to the author?

Centers for Disease Control and Prevention, "Guidelines for National Human Immunodeficiency Virus Case Surveillance, Including Monitoring for Human Immunodeficiency Virus Infection and Acquired Immunodeficiency Syndrome," *Morbidity and Mortality Recommendations and Reports*, December 10, 1999.

A IDS surveillance has been the cornerstone of national efforts to monitor the spread of HIV infection in the United States and to target HIV-prevention programs and health-care services. Although AIDS is the end-stage of the natural history of HIV infection, in the past, monitoring AIDS-defining conditions provided population-based data that reflected changes in the incidence of HIV infection. However, recent advances in HIV treatment have slowed the progression of HIV disease for infected persons on treatment and contributed to a decline in AIDS incidence. These advances in treatment have diminished the ability of AIDS surveillance data to represent trends in the incidence of HIV infection or the impact of the epidemic on the health-care system. As a consequence, the capacity of local, state, and federal public health agencies to monitor the HIV epidemic has been compromised.

In response to these changes and following consultations with multiple and diverse constituencies (including representatives of public health, government, and community organizations), Centers for Disease Control and Prevention (CDC) and the Council of State and Territorial Epidemiologists (CSTE) have recommended that all states and territories include surveillance for HIV infection as an extension of their AIDS surveillance activities. In this manner, the HIV/AIDS epidemic can be tracked more accurately and appropriate information about HIV infection and AIDS can be made available to policymakers. CDC continues to support a diverse set of epidemiologic methods to characterize persons affected by the epidemic in the United States. Although HIV/AIDS case surveillance represents only one component among multiple necessary surveillance strategies, this report focuses primarily on CDC's recommendation to implement HIV case reporting nationwide. . . .

History of HIV/AIDS Surveillance

Since the epidemic was first identified in the United States in 1981, population-based AIDS surveillance (i.e., reporting of AIDS cases and their characteristics to public health authorities for epidemiologic analysis) has been used to track the progression of the HIV epidemic from the initial case reports of opportunistic illnesses caused by a then unknown agent in a few large cities to the reporting of 711,344 AIDS cases nationwide through June 30, 1999. The AIDS reporting criteria have been periodically revised to incorporate new understanding of HIV disease and changes in medical practice. In the absence of effective therapy for HIV infection, AIDS surveillance data have reliably detected changing patterns of HIV transmission and reflected the effect of HIV-prevention programs on the incidence of HIV infection and related illnesses in specific populations. Because of these attributes, AIDS surveillance data have been used as a basis for allocating many federal resources for HIV treatment and care services and as the epidemiologic basis for planning local HIV-prevention services.

With the advent of more effective therapy that slows the progression of HIV disease, AIDS surveillance data no longer reliably reflect trends in HIV transmission and do not accurately represent the need for prevention and care services. In 1996, national AIDS incidence and AIDS deaths declined for the first time during the HIV epidemic. . . .

In contrast to AIDS case surveillance, HIV case surveillance provides data to better characterize populations in which HIV infection has been newly diagnosed, including persons with evidence of recent HIV infection such as adolescents and young adults (13–24-year-olds). Of the 52,690 HIV infections diagnosed from January 1994 through June 1997 in 25 states that conducted name-based HIV surveillance throughout this period, 14% of cases occurred in persons aged 13–24 years. In comparison, of the 20,215 persons in whom AIDS was diagnosed in these 25 states, only 3% of cases occurred in persons aged 13–24 years. Thus, AIDS case surveillance alone does not accurately reflect the extent of the HIV epidemic among adolescents and young adults. Compared with persons reported with AIDS, those reported with HIV infection in these 25 states were more likely to be women and from racial/ethnic minorities. . . .

HIV Testing Strategies

Persons can choose to be tested for HIV in the following ways: a) anonymously—whereby identifying information,

HIV Reporting Required **Pediatric Reporting Required Only**

Centers for Disease Control and Prevention, *MMWR*, December 10, 1999.

including patient name and other locating information, are not linked to the HIV test result (e.g., at anonymous testing sites) and b) confidentially—whereby the HIV test result is linked to identifying information such as patient and provider names (e.g., at medical clinics). In states that require HIV case reporting, providers in confidential medical or testing sites are required to report HIV-infected persons to public health authorities. Not all persons infected with HIV are tested, and of those who are, testing occurs at different stages of their infection. Therefore, HIV surveillance data provide a minimum estimate of the number of infected persons and are most representative of persons who have had HIV infection diagnosed in medical clinics and other confidential diagnostic settings. The data represent the characteristics of persons who recognize their risk and seek confidential testing, who are offered HIV testing (e.g., pregnant women and clients at sexually transmitted disease [STD] clinics), who are required to be tested (e.g., blood donors and military recruits), and who are tested because they present with symptoms of HIV-related illnesses. CDC estimated that, in 1996, approximately two thirds of all infected persons in the United States had HIV infection diagnosed in such settings. HIV surveillance data might not represent untested persons or those who seek testing at anonymous test sites or with home collection kits; such persons are not reported to confidential HIV/AIDS surveillance systems. However, the availability of anonymous testing is important in promoting knowledge of HIV status among at-risk populations and provides an opportunity for counseling to reduce high-risk behaviors and voluntary referrals to appropriate medical diagnosis and prevention services.

Despite their current limitations, HIV and AIDS case surveillance data together can provide a clearer picture of the HIV epidemic than AIDS case surveillance data alone. Therefore, CDC and CSTE continue to recommend that all areas implement HIV case reporting as part of a comprehensive strategy to monitor HIV infection and HIV disease. The strategy should also include surveys of the incidence and prevalence of HIV infection; AIDS case surveillance; monitoring HIV-related mortality; supplemental research and evaluation studies, including behavioral surveillance; and statistical estimation of the incidence and prevalence of infection and disease. . . .

HIV Surveillance and Testing Behavior

Few studies have characterized test- or care-seeking behaviors in relation to state HIV reporting policies. A 1988 general population study of previous or planned use of HIV testing services did not identify an association of reporting policy with testing behavior. In contrast, interviews of persons seeking anonymous testing in 1989 documented that many would avoid testing if a positive test resulted in name reporting or partner notification. A review of the published literature on HIV testing behaviors highlighted several limitations and biases in previous studies, including small numbers, lack of geographic and risk-group representativeness, and analysis of intent to test rather than of actual testing behavior. An additional limitation of the available literature is that studies published 5–10 years ago might not reflect actual testing behaviors in the current treatment era. Literature that highlights potential misuse of public health surveillance data might have the unintended effect of increasing test avoidance among some at-risk persons. Examining knowledge of and perceptions about testing and reporting, as well as actual testing behavior, in the context of current treatment advances and evolving HIV reporting policies, can address some of the limitations of previous research.

To determine the effect of changes in reporting policies on actual testing behaviors among persons seeking testing at publicly funded HIV counseling and testing sites, CDC and six state health departments reviewed data routinely collected from these sites to compare HIV testing patterns during the 12 months before and the 12 months after implementation of HIV case surveillance. In these areas, the number of HIV tests increased in four states and decreased in two states; the declines were not statistically significant. All the analysis periods (25-month periods during 1992–1996) antedated the widespread beneficial effects of highly active antiretroviral therapy. Slight variability in testing trends was observed among racial/ethnic subgroups and HIV-risk exposure categories; however, these data do not suggest that, in these states, the policy of implementing HIV case reporting adversely affected test-seeking behaviors overall.

Test Avoidance

CDC also supported studies by researchers at the University of California at San Francisco and participating state health departments to identify the most important determinants of test seeking or test avoidance among high-risk populations and to assess the impact of changes in HIV testing and HIV reporting policies. Data from these surveys of high-risk persons in nine selected states about their perceptions and knowledge of HIV testing and HIV reporting practices documented that few respondents had knowledge of the HIV reporting policies in their respective states. In surveys conducted during 1995–1996, respondents reported high levels of testing, with approximately three fourths reporting that they had had an HIV test. The most commonly reported factors (by nearly half of respondents) that might have contributed to delays in seeking testing or not getting tested were fear of having HIV infection diagnosed or belief that they were not likely to be HIV infected. "Reporting to the government" was a concern that might have contributed to a delay in seeking HIV testing for 11% of heterosexuals, 18% of injecting-drug users, and 22% of men who have sex with men; less than 1%, 3%, and 2% of respondents in these risk groups, respectively, indicated that this was their main concern. Concern about name-based reporting of HIV infections to the government was a factor for not testing for HIV for 13% of heterosexuals, 18% of injecting-drug users, and 28% of men who have sex with men. As the main factor for not testing for HIV, concern about name-based reporting to the government was substantially lower in all risk groups (1% of heterosexuals, 1% of injecting-drug users, and 4% of men who have sex with men). These findings suggest that name-based reporting policies might deter a small proportion of persons with high-risk sex or drug-using behaviors from seeking testing and, therefore, support the need for strict adherence to confidentiality safeguards of public health testing and surveillance data. In addition, the survey documented that the availability of an anonymous testing option is consistently associated with higher rates of intention to test in the future. In this survey, high levels of testing, together with high levels of test delay or avoidance associated with reasons other than concern about name reporting, suggest that addressing these other concerns may have a greater effect on testing behavior. For example, 59% of men who have sex with men reported being "afraid to find out" as a factor for not testing, and 27% reported it as the main factor for not testing. In addition, 52% of men who have sex with men reported "unlikely to have been exposed" as a factor for not testing, and 17% reported it as the main factor.

In a companion survey of persons reported with AIDS in eight of these same states, participants who had recognized their HIV risk and sought testing at anonymous testing sites reported entering care at an earlier stage of HIV disease than persons who were first tested in a confidential testing setting (e.g., STD clinics, medical clinics, or hospitals), where persons are frequently first tested when they become ill. These data suggest that anonymous testing options are important in promoting timely knowledge of HIV status for some at-risk persons.

"We do not believe that the benefits of names reporting outweigh the potential deterrence from HIV testing and/or treatment."

Names Reporting of HIV Infection Deters Testing

San Francisco AIDS Foundation

In the following viewpoint, the San Francisco AIDS Foundation (SFAF) argues that mandatory names reporting—the providing of names of those who test positive for HIV to health departments—will deter people from testing for HIV. Studies and surveys have found that people will avoid or delay getting tested for HIV if their positive results will be reported to the government. This delay in testing, the organization maintains, means that HIV-positive people would not get the care and treatment they need to stay healthy. The SFAF contends that HIV tests that use a unique code to identify people will allow the government to track the disease without infringing on people's right to privacy. The San Francisco AIDS Foundation helps people living with HIV and AIDS, provides information about the disease, and develops public policy recommendations for state and federal governments.

As you read, consider the following questions:
1. How many people infected with HIV do not know they are infected, according to the Centers for Disease Control?
2. According to the San Francisco AIDS Foundation, what states currently use or are considering unique identifiers for their HIV tests?

An HIV test is the first step a person must take to learn their health status, and take appropriate measures to stay healthy. However, the federal Centers for Disease Control & Prevention (CDC) estimates that over a third of those infected in the U.S. do not know their HIV status. The current clinical guidelines recommend initiating care as early in the course of disease as possible to obtain the maximum benefit. Therefore, people at risk for HIV infection should be encouraged to find out their HIV status as soon as possible after exposure to make informed treatment decisions, and any barriers to testing should be removed as quickly as possible.

Changes in the epidemic have led to increasing concern that existing AIDS surveillance efforts are becoming outdated, and a call for an expanded HIV reporting system. The San Francisco AIDS Foundation acknowledges the need for improved HIV data. However, we strongly disagree that HIV names reporting is necessary, and we do not believe that the benefits of names reporting outweigh the potential deterrence from HIV testing and/or treatment.

Names Reporting Deters Testing

Research on the impact of mandatory names reporting on testing has shown that:

• A 1997 study in anonymous test sites in San Francisco found that 68% said they would not be willing to get tested if their name would be reported to the government.

• The 1996 HIV Testing Survey (HITS) showed that 19% of those surveyed who had never been tested said that the fear that their name might be reported to the government was a factor in their decision not to get tested, after reasons such as fear of finding out, or believing that they were not at risk. For 2% fear of reporting was the main reason.

• The same survey reported that 18% of those who had delayed testing did so because of fear of being reported to the government, with 3% citing it as the main reason.

• A 1995 survey done in HIV testing centers in Los Angeles showed that 86% of participants would not have been tested if they knew that their name would be reported to the government.

• A 1989 study in California reported that over 60% of

individuals would not get tested if the results were reported.

An AIDS Health Project survey in San Francisco shows that when names reporting is explained, the deterrent effect is reduced somewhat, but the majority of individuals still indicated that they would avoid testing if names reporting were implemented:

• Of the 68% who said they would not get tested if their name were reported, 12% changed their minds about getting tested once the public health benefits of reporting were explained to them, but a 58% majority continued to oppose testing.

• If the benefits were explained before the question about testing was asked, 46% reported that they would not test if names were reported.

A 1998 survey of clients of the San Francisco AIDS Foundation found that 33% of clients would have avoided testing and another 11% would have delayed it if their name were reported confidentially to a government health agency.

Few people in the HITS study reported that their worries about names reporting were the main reason they had not gotten tested earlier, but a significant number said that it had an effect on their decision. The main reasons they did not test were that they were afraid to find out, that they thought they were not at risk, or that they didn't want to think about it. Those are all very personal reasons, which anyone getting tested must consider. Although education campaigns or good counseling can help individuals think through these barriers, they are not the result of a governmental action. The reporting of names, however, is the one cause of delayed or avoided testing, which the government can eliminate, by not asking for names as HIV surveillance.

The HITS study also shows that some individuals may not know whether or not their state requires names reporting. However, a lack of information on names reporting policies does not imply that those policies will have no effect on behavior once people learn what the relevant policies are in their states. Individuals should have adequate information about the policies in effect in their state when they choose to be tested so that they may make informed decisions regarding HIV testing.

The studies cited here may disagree on the degree of deterrence to testing, but they all reflect some level of deterrence.

High Risk Groups

Research has shown a strong deterrent effect in groups which are at high risk for infection, and when high risk groups have been compared to lower risk groups, the deterrent effect is higher for those groups at highest risk. It is also high among communities which have been disproportionately affected by HIV infection, including gay/bisexual men, African-Americans and Latinos. Many of the groups at highest risk for infection, including injection drug users, sex workers, men who have sex with men, and groups which have disproportionate rates of infection, such as African-Americans and Latinos, have a long-standing (and in many cases reasonable) distrust of government, and names reporting would only exacerbate those concerns.

- A 1989 study from UCSF showed that names reporting would reduce the number of gay/bisexual men willing to be tested.

- Other studies have shown that names reporting would have a significant impact on African-American and Latino testing rates.

- In South Carolina, when anonymous testing was ended, the number of gay men getting tested dropped by 51%. HIV positive results dropped by 43%, suggesting that many of those who were positive were not getting tested at all.

- In a 1992 survey 77% of gay & bisexual men reported that not wanting their name to be on a government list was one of the most important reasons for not getting tested.

- A 1994 study in Arizona showed that men who have sex with men delayed testing until anonymous testing was available due to a fear of being reported. It also showed a significantly higher rate of HIV infection among those who delayed testing.

Access to Treatment Is Delayed

Names reporting would also deter individuals with HIV from accessing medical treatment for their HIV infection. The available research shows that:

• In the Los Angeles survey, 23% of those getting tested said that they would not access medical care until they became sick, if name-based reporting were implemented.

• In the same study, when individuals who were HIV-positive were asked what they would have done had their names been reported when they accessed care, 25% said that they would have waited until they were sick, and another 36% said that they might not have accessed treatment at all.

• The AIDS Patient Survey showed that people access care later in states with names reporting than in states without it. Specifically, CD4 counts were significantly lower in names reporting than non-names reporting states.

• In the same study, of those who delayed accessing care more than a month after testing positive, 10% cited fear of being reported to the government as a reason.

• The San Francisco AIDS Foundation 1998 Client Survey found that 12% of those surveyed said they might not have sought treatment if they knew that their name would be reported to health officials when they sought medical care, and another 29% said they would not have sought treatment unless they were very sick.

Who Gets the Names?

Names reporting is important to some and not to others. But what does names reporting and expanded surveillance actually mean? If it means that when I test for HIV, my name is reported to the Health Department and that's the end of it, . . . well, fine. But, if it means that I test positive and then I get a knock on the door from a public health field officer inquiring about what actions I've taken, and what the names of my sex partners are, that's not OK. Or, if I get a call at work wanting to know where I receive my care, or have my children been tested?, and if I refuse to answer them, and I have not accessed care, and then child protective services is contacted and then I lose my children; that is definitely not O.K.

Mary Lucey, *Women Alive*, Summer 1998.

The success of new combination treatments has been used as a justification for names reporting, on the grounds that names reporting will somehow ensure access to treatments, and that expanded surveillance is needed to compensate for people with HIV not getting sick enough to be diagnosed with AIDS. In fact, one of the largest implications of the new treatments is that everyone infected with HIV should enter care as soon as possible in the course of infection, and to do that, they must know their HIV status. If names reporting serves as a barrier to testing, then we lose more than we gain. A better understanding of the epidemic is important, but not at the cost of expanding the epidemic.

Unique Identifiers

The primary HIV surveillance system that is considered an alternative to names reporting is unique identifier reporting. Under such a system, an HIV-infected individual would not be reported by name to public health officials but rather by some form of a unique code that could not be traced back to the person. Unique identifiers would address some of the confidentiality concerns and HIV testing deterrence caused by name-based reporting, and still help meet the need for improved surveillance of HIV disease.

Unique identifier reporting has been seen as a potential compromise between those who strongly believe that better HIV data is needed and those who have strong public health and privacy concerns regarding HIV names reporting. Unique identifiers, if designed and implemented properly, are as specific as names in enabling unduplicated counts of people living with HIV, yet do not create a list that could potentially be used to identify individuals. Unique identifiers are currently in use in Maryland, and are being implemented or actively considered in a number of other states, including Massachusetts, Illinois, Hawaii, and California.

"Many people have been needlessly infected because leadership shirked its responsibility to use trained interviewers and investigators to elicit and trace [the sexual] contacts [of people who have AIDS]."

Partner Notification of HIV Status Should Be Mandatory

William B. Kaliher

William B. Kaliher has investigated cases of venereal disease for more than twenty-five years. In the following viewpoint, Kaliher asserts that while it is mandatory for health departments to find and notify the sexual partners of patients with venereal disease, partner notification in HIV cases is not mandatory. He argues that partner notification is especially important in HIV/AIDS cases, however, as AIDS is always fatal. Without mandatory notification, he contends that those who have HIV can continue to infect other people. If people with HIV/AIDS are notified that they may be infected, they can get tested.

As you read, consider the following questions:
1. In Kaliher's opinion, why is South Carolina's AIDS program far superior to all other states' programs?
2. According to Kaliher, how do health educators duplicate media efforts regarding HIV/AIDS?
3. Who, according to the author, are the groups that are most at risk for contracting HIV?

William B. Kaliher, "How Federal and State Policies Spread AIDS," *World & I*, June 1998. Copyright © 1998 by News World Communications, Inc. Reproduced with permission.

I am one of the few venereal disease investigators, if not the only one, who has been allowed to interview HIV-positive patients and trace HIV/AIDS contacts since 1985. I have observed many aspects of this disease not reported to the general public, and I have managed the case investigations of over nine hundred infected patients. We properly interviewed the majority of those individuals.

Not in the Interest of Public Health

My twenty-five years' experience working with venereal diseases and my involvement in this aspect of AIDS has made me acutely aware of and concerned over the illogical public health decisions concerning AIDS. Scrutinizing the Centers for Disease Control and Prevention (CDC), one could conclude that this agency is concealing certain facts from the public, or one could think, as a respected doctor said after working at the CDC, "Every decision is being politically made." No matter your personal perspective, two observations are painfully clear: It is apparent decisions are not being made in the interest of public health, if that goal means retarding the spread of communicable diseases, and the decisions made are not maximizing the benefits from the public's tax dollars.

A venereal disease investigator appears to have the straightforward job of interviewing infected persons and bringing their contacts in for treatment. But the detective-like qualities of an experienced investigator allow intervention in more dramatic ways. In my area of South Carolina, with AIDS the above description is fairly accurate, except we bring the contacts in for counseling and testing by nurses instead of treatment. Unfortunately, for the American taxpayer and—more importantly—the people at risk, we are virtually the only area in the United States since 1985 that has dealt with AIDS as a communicable disease. Tabulation files of HIV/AIDS contacts are not being kept in any adequate way nationally.

An Example of the Problem

A dramatic method of disease intervention and unpardonable problems with the national AIDS program is demonstrated by the case of a thirty-year-old non-IV-drug-using, HIV-positive heterosexual female. I describe her by her lack of risk factors because she was diagnosed when women without risk factors were being ignored, avoided, or thought to be anomalies. She named four men as sexual contacts in the five years prior to her positive test. One contact, a one-night stand, was not located. A second was tested and found HIV-negative. Information concerning a third man who had been fired from a bottling plant, was forwarded to another city. Because of our program structure, that was the end of his AIDS investigation. Had he been a syphilis contact, the investigators would have obtained his address from the company and traced him.

Her fourth contact, an alcoholic heterosexual, was located two months after being named. When tested, he was found to be EIA positive and western blot indeterminate, meaning another test was needed to determine if he was actually infected. While awaiting his initial test results, this man decided he did not want to be followed. With many less-dangerous STDs (sexually transmitted diseases), he could not legally refuse testing and possibly other follow-up, but with AIDS testing, that option was his right.

We tried to obtain a second and conclusive test, but he avoided us for over a year. On the occasions when we located him, he refused further testing. We eventually did what is called a cluster interview of the infected woman who named him. She identified two other women he was having sex with. We also learned of two additional women he was involved with during visits to his parents' home. In total, we discovered four other heterosexual contacts of this man's without interviewing him or having a positive test. Three of the four women tested positive. Two of those named over twenty contacts each, with one of them having already spread the disease to two other men.

Three years after we located those four women, two other women were incidentally tested and found to be positive for HIV. They named this man, but we lack either the laws or more probably the leadership with the will to force this man to be tested and/or stop him from infecting others. The incidents concerning this case became known in 1989. In 1992 an additional four people who related directly to the original patients in this case had become infected, demonstrating the problems of controlling a communicable disease without having a program with "real objectives" and a clear, methodical method of tracing contacts.

Inexperienced Leadership and Homosexual Lobbying

In many states, virtually anybody except physicians, nurses, venereal disease investigators, or epidemiologists was selected to manage AIDS programs. The selection of inexperienced leadership combined with homosexual lobbying resulted in many states lacking the essentials of a disease-control program. Name-reporting systems were often nonexistent. Anonymous reporting was encouraged. Accountability mechanisms to ensure patients were contacted and—even in the best-managed states—exceedingly poor interviewing and contact-tracing programs were put in place. Despite such poor quality, South Carolina has a program that is considered one of the nation's best. Its accomplishments in reducing the spread of AIDS have been achieved by local efforts, not necessarily because of state leadership and definitely in spite of national leadership.

Nationally, proper interviews that could lead to disease intervention are not routinely obtained, and contacts are rarely followed. Nurses or counselors in most states were assigned the role of conducting intense interviews for sexual contacts without adequate training. In addition to their lack of training, these workers were not allowed to gain those skills by doing in-depth interviews on gonorrhea patients to determine what they could produce.

The results of such mindless experiments in disease control with perhaps the most dangerous disease of the century have been disastrous. A study by doctors at the University of North Carolina, published in the *New England Journal of Medicine*, and reported on by newspapers in January 1992, revealed the horrors and depth of the problem of having a national AIDS program in name only. They discovered that counselors located only half of all partners named, while infected people told only 7 percent of the people they exposed.

Of the 534 people studied, almost half never returned to the clinic. Of the partners notified during the study, 94 percent were unaware they had been exposed to the virus.

Factors as basic as contact indexes, number of locatable contacts, and the number of cases relating to other infected individuals were not considered. Often those in charge of programs did not know the meaning of such basic terms or concepts. The ability to systematically transmit contact information from one county or state to another or to an accounting system to ensure every AIDS patient was either counseled or interviewed is still lacking.

It should have been obvious from the start, as poor results readily demonstrated, that a nurse could not properly conduct a quality sexual interview—pushing for hidden contacts—and still function as a nurse giving nurturing care to the same infected individual. Taking a gentle view, this was, and is, the philosophy of leadership guiding most programs in the nation, a leadership that has never wanted to examine facts and productivity or base decisions on such mundane reasoning. A leadership that in one small city allowed or caused hundreds of positive test results to be lost. Four years later, with no changes having been made, the same error recurred. Another hundred positive reports were discovered in a desk drawer. The positive HIV reports were simply set aside and ignored. The patients involved were never notified. This is only one minor example of our country's AIDS programs. Should you think it couldn't be worse, then consider that during the past thirteen years [since 1985] most states have lacked programs that could even gather the hundred positive reports by name and address. The reason South Carolina's AIDS program is far superior to most is self-explanatory: There is little else adequate for comparison.

Ineffective Health Education

Exacerbating matters for the tax-paying public, the health educator contingent duplicates the media with their efforts. For thirteen years newspapers and TV have almost daily delivered facts concerning AIDS. One cannot imagine a normal human being in the United States being unaware of the three ways that the CDC claims AIDS is spread. Infected people with an IQ of sixty can explain how AIDS is spread. Despite this public awareness, health educators are still designing programs to reemphasize such basic knowledge during prime-time TV hours.

NO TESTING WILL DRIVE AIDS CARRIERS UNDERGROUND

Shelton. © 1987 by *The Orange County Register*. Reprinted with permission.

At some point the leaders in the war on AIDS should realize that people sitting home watching TV are not the most at-risk groups. Instead of working on their standard pamphlets and TV productions, health educators should travel to areas where crack users live and deal, where women perform oral sex on as many as fifteen men an evening. Perhaps then they could discover a more at-risk population and design more-effective messages. By ignoring these groups, educators find little to say beyond their standard messages. Such staid thinking abounds among our leadership.

In my small area of South Carolina, without bias and without a hidden agenda, our staff has for the most part been able to attack AIDS as a communicable disease. With data collection, the chips have fallen as they should. For thirteen years we have consistently found that nearly 35 percent of our HIV-positive people are heterosexual, non-IV drug users—a finding quite different from what has been nationally indicated. One woman has heterosexually infected nine men. This information has been known for ten years, and yet the CDC has never officially inquired how this happened or asked if we had similar cases. The case was discussed in the national news and still prompted no inquiry from either the CDC or the state AIDS program. Private physicians, such as Dr. J.D. Robinson, did inquire into these heterosexual cases, but these are not the people running the CDC. Those who inquired from the CDC have done so only unofficially.

Our basic data compiled in 1990 included the following information: of 203 infected individuals identified, 23 refused to name any contacts, but 180 named 836 contacts. (I am including cluster contacts with contacts to simplify this report, but the cluster numbers were not significant enough to alter the findings.) Of the 836 contacts, 116 tested positive and 404 were negative (in other words, about 20 percent of those tested were positive). The remainder either lived outside my area and were not checked or are pending. Some 92 of the 836 contacts lived in states that will not notify them—a good cause for virtually everyone to feel less secure.

Prolonging Lives and Deterring AIDS

We who follow AIDS as a venereal disease make many observations that will be verified in time. If sexual contacts are notified and found to be positive in the early stage of the infection, they are able to immediately begin good nutritional habits as well as monitor their health before becoming sick. We estimate that with this process patients can prolong their lives in a healthy state for at least three years longer than people who find they are infected after becoming ill. Also, by discovering their infection earlier than they would have without a partner notification program, they can avoid unintentionally spreading the infection to others.

A realistic review of the ever-increasing number of babies being born to HIV-positive mothers should signal much greater concern than has been aroused. This increase in infected babies clearly demonstrates how inaccurate CDC assumptions and predictions have been. If you consider that most women who know they are infected do not get pregnant, then the constantly climbing figure for perinatal infection becomes more alarming. This indicates that the real heterosexual AIDS or HIV increase may be far larger than is imagined.

Many areas of AIDS infection seem paradoxical. One person may be exposed once or twice and become infected, while another with multiple exposures remains HIV-negative. This is not in the majority of cases, but it occurs enough to make one wonder. We see a healthy person deteriorate rapidly and a sickly person survive much longer than expected. Two people with T-cell counts of zero for over a year did well. We wondered why no one studies these apparent survivors. Do they have some unknown genetic makeup that allows them to remain healthy enough to work every day—and without medication?

Obviously, the AIDS program should have been put in the proper hands years ago. Many people have been needlessly infected because leadership shirked its responsibility to use trained interviewers and investigators to elicit and trace contacts and to require the testing of contacts. How can supposedly sane leaders have failed to push for laws to incarcerate the small percentage of infected individuals who have intentionally spread this infection? Many of the private AIDS organizations do no better in halting the disease. In June 1991, the International AIDS Society mailed an urgent letter asking people to write legislators and certain other individuals to protest the U.S. ban that kept infected individuals from entering our country. This group made itself into a political advocacy group and attempted to influence policy for political reasons, not medical ones. It also encouraged an international boycott against allowing any international AIDS conference to be held in the United States. Not a word in the letter mentioned doing anything to halt the spread of the disease. Could they possibly imagine that something as basic as reporting positively tested individuals by name might be important in slowing the spread of AIDS?

Too often, HIV-positive individuals return to the clinic with gonorrhea, signifying that they are not practicing safe sex but are spreading AIDS. A mind-boggling amount of AIDS or HIV virus can be spread in the pus from gonorrheal discharge during sex—a discharge loaded with white [blood] cells, the home of the virus.

How can the current leadership be allowed to stay in control of the AIDS program? Is there no one who can be held accountable when many infected people are not notified? Can anyone be held responsible for the AIDS program being totally ineffective in slowing the disease's spread? The sad reality is that when AIDS programs falsely give the appearance of working toward controlling the disease, they protect themselves from being properly monitored and thereby actually help spread the disease.

Secrecy Must Go

The other side of the AIDS disease control question must be brought out. Secrecy should never be allowed in nonmilitary, tax-supported organizations. More public health employees would gladly speak out to condemn the national AIDS effort, but they fear losing their jobs. Two health officers in New York City paid the price for trying to build a real AIDS program. We saw a national uproar over Darnell McGee, who infected at least eighteen women in Missouri, and over Nessbawn Williams, who infected at least nine women in Mayville, New York. Several years ago there was a similar uproar over Edward Savitz exposing children to AIDS in Philadelphia. But unknown to the public, some workers have questioned the AIDS leadership and even accused them of knowingly making decisions that would ensure the continued destructive behavior of the McGees and the Savitzes of this world.

Last but not least, it is time to separate AIDS control from the homosexual agenda. There is no difference between a Klansman hiding his sheets during the day while appearing to work for civil rights and a closeted queen health official pretending to work for disease control while ensuring the opposite. It is past time we add disease intervention to the title of the AIDS program. The current omission of these words tells the story.

"The available evidence does not support the assumption that partners who are notified and tested reduce high-risk behavior or receive effective treatment, thus reducing transmission of HIV."

Partner Notification of HIV Status Should Not Be Mandatory

American Civil Liberties Union

The American Civil Liberties Union (ACLU) argues in the following viewpoint that partner notification programs—programs that notify the sexual partners of people infected with a venereal disease—are ineffective in controlling the spread of HIV/AIDS. Nor is there evidence that those who have been notified and tested for HIV change their high-risk behavior. In addition, the ACLU asserts that many people refuse to name their sexual partners due to fears of stigma and discrimination. The ACLU is a national organization that works to defend civil rights guaranteed by the U.S. Constitution.

As you read, consider the following questions:

1. What are the two false assumptions made about partner notification as a proven tool of prevention, in the author's opinion?
2. What is the fundamental difference between a sexually transmitted disease like syphilis and HIV, according to the ACLU?

The term "partner notification" refers to activities aimed at identifying sex and/or needlesharing partners of someone with a disease communicable through sex or shared needles and informing them that they have been exposed to the disease. Little empirical work exists that effectively evaluates the costs and benefits of partner notification. Voluntary partner notification plans, which encourage an infected individual to notify his or her partners and provide training and support, are one component of effective HIV prevention and treatment. However, the available evidence does not justify coercive partner notification. Instead, the scientific research shows that partner notification that is not voluntary or that is linked to HIV surveillance through name reporting will not work.

In the "traditional" context of partner notification for control of sexually transmitted diseases (STDs), partner notification programs have frequently failed. Partner notification has not been effective in controlling recent STD outbreaks which are the result of high-risk activities similar to those driving the largest number of new cases of HIV infection. The evidence also shows that partner notification does little to change the high risk behavior of those most likely to contract HIV. At the same time, coercive partner notification diverts resources from programs that do work. Resources for treatment and prevention services, which result in more people being treated more effectively and fewer people becoming infected, are already insufficient.

The ACLU recognizes that it is extremely important that individuals who test positive for HIV notify any partners who have been placed at risk. The ACLU therefore supports voluntary partner notification plans. But the ACLU adamantly opposes state-mandated coercive partner notification, including plans that require individuals with HIV to provide the names of their partners to public health authorities and/or require public health authorities to notify partners without the consent of the patient.

Breaking the Chain of Transmission

Partner notification emerged as a public health tool in the United States in the 1930's. The rationale behind partner notification is that it allows identification, treatment, and education of individuals who have been exposed to a communicable disease, preventing the spread of the disease and helping people understand how to avoid future infection. After the discovery of penicillin as a cure of gonorrhea and syphilis, partner notification became a standard strategy for breaking the chain of transmission of those and other diseases. Partners were contacted by public health officers and immediately treated so that they could not infect others.

Partner notification has not been used systematically with HIV. There are several reasons for this: lack of a drug therapy to cure HIV or prevent transmission, a long incubation period which makes it difficult for patients to name and locate past partners, and serious concerns about confidentiality and social stigma. For these reasons, there has been broad consensus that coercive partner notification is not warranted with HIV.

Recent calls for aggressive and coercive partner notification have been fueled at least in part by the development of drug therapies for treating HIV. These therapies are helping people with HIV live longer and healthier lives. Research suggests that the new drug therapies may be more effective if begun soon after infection. However, the new drug therapies do not offer a cure, and individuals under treatment can still infect others.

Another factor that has changed in recent years is the demographics of HIV. While gay and bisexual men made up the largest at-risk population in the first decade of the AIDS epidemic, in the second decade new cases of HIV are increasingly occurring among people of color and injection drug users. Educational outreach to these groups has been more difficult and less effective than it was in gay communities, and partner notification has been suggested by some as an alternative to targeted prevention education. At the same time, frank, culturally appropriate education and counseling and other prevention measures, such as needle exchange and drug treatment have been largely ignored or rejected on ideological grounds. . . .

Many calls for coercive, state-mandated partner notification policies are based on claims that partner notification is

Mandatory Partner Notification Is Ineffective

Applied on a voluntary basis (i.e., when the infected patient has given explicit consent to notification of partners either by her/himself or by the health provider) partner notification is an important way of protecting the uninfected partner, providing the information necessary to take protective action and an opportunity for education for prevention. It is also an important way of helping the already infected partner in terms of access to early treatment and care. Voluntary and confidential partner notification should be part of the standard of HIV/AIDS care, accompanied by psychosocial and medical care and support, including counselling, in a supportive environment which provides legal, material and social protection from negative consequences of disclosure.

Public health experience in control of sexually transmitted infections shows that partner notification carried out mandatorily is a relatively ineffective means of "breaking the chain of transmission" when there is considerable delay before contacts can be traced, when sex with partners other than the regular partner is common, and when health services are inaccessible or unacceptable to clients. These are lessons which can be applied to HIV infection which has a very long incubation period and is often associated with sex outside primary relationships.

World Health Organization, "Questions and Answers on Reporting, Partner Notification, and Disclosure of HIV Serostatus and/or AIDS—Public Health and Human Rights Implications," June 1999.

a "traditional" public health tool used to prevent the spread of STDs. Proponents of coercive partner notification for HIV argue that public health efforts to prevent the spread of HIV must use such "proven tools" of prevention. But this argument makes at least two false assumptions: 1) that coercive partner notification measures that are being implemented or proposed in the context of HIV infection are similar to "traditional" public health strategies; and 2) that "traditional" strategies have been effective in controlling other communicable diseases.

Programs Must Be Confidential and Voluntary

Partner notification strategies that abandon anonymity and attempt to coerce participation in notification entail "a rejection of the lessons of four decades of contact tracing, lessons that were rooted in the pragmatics of STD control," according to researchers Ronald Bayer and Kathleen E. Toomey.

When partner notification was first considered as a public health tool to fight the spread of STDs, there was great debate about names based case reporting and coercive partner notification for "traditional" disease prevention. Even though this debate occurred prior to the development of our modern understanding of the importance of privacy as a right, there was strong support for maintaining the anonymity of patients diagnosed with STDs and designing programs that would encourage patients to participate voluntarily in the public health system. The ability of a person infected with an STD to maintain his or her anonymity while receiving treatment and counseling has always been, and remains, an important part of the public health equation for determining appropriate methods of disease prevention.

In part, this reflects an obvious reality: no matter what a law says, as a practical matter, no one can be forced to provide information about sexual or needle-sharing partners if he or she is not willing to do so. Thus, while partner notification has always been susceptible to coercive tactics, the necessity of voluntary cooperation of an infected person in notifying his or her partners has not been disputed in traditional public health strategies. . . .

The Basic Failings of Partner Notification

A 1996 review of the evidence available on the effectiveness of partner notification in controlling STDs points out the basic failings. The study concludes that partner notification is a relatively ineffective means of disease control when sex with anonymous partners is common, when there is considerable delay before contacts can be traced, and when health services are inaccessible or unacceptable to clients. Notably, these factors have been among the most prevalent characteristics of the AIDS epidemic. The report also notes that "[s]trikingly absent from the literature are any community-based comparison studies which attempt to evaluate the effectiveness of partner notification in reducing the incidence or prevalence of disease in the community." Instead, the success of partner notification has been evaluated in terms of the percentage of named partners that are ultimately notified, which, as the Oregon study notes, is not meaningful when only a small percentage of total exposed partners are likely to be identified in the first place.

However, the most serious failure of partner notification is not its inability to find people exposed, but its deterrent effect on testing and treatment. It is true of course that STD partner notification programs have led to the testing and treatment of some individuals who might otherwise have gone untreated. But this has come at a significant cost, since partner notification programs have also caused some individuals to avoid being tested for STDs out of fear that they would be asked or required to give information about their sexual contacts. These individuals, who would otherwise have received treatment, most likely have instead infected others. And, of course, there has been no partner notification in these cases since there was no STD diagnosis in the first instance.

Even Less Effective for HIV

There is a fundamental difference between an STD like syphilis on the one hand and HIV on the other—namely, the existence of a medical treatment that renders an infected individual uninfectious. Such a treatment exists for syphilis, but not for HIV. Therefore, partner notification programs have a far greater chance of breaking the chain of transmission with syphilis than with HIV.

In addition, the various risk factors that have been attributed to the failure of partner notification efforts in controlling recent outbreaks of syphilis—drug dependency, anonymous sex, needle-sharing partners, and the exchange of sex for drugs or money—are all present among the fastest growing population at risk for contracting HIV.

Moreover, from the early years of the AIDS epidemic, there has been widespread recognition that absent any therapy which eliminates one individual's ability to infect another, a successful response to the epidemic was unavoidably dependent on the willingness of those at risk for infection to voluntarily comply with public health messages. HIV public health policy is largely based on encouraging people at high risk of contracting HIV to voluntarily seek testing and modify risky behavior. Voluntary testing and acceptance of public health messages require that those at risk trust and cooperate with public health. And it has long been recognized that coercive strategies such as involuntary partner notification will erode this trust and cooperation.

Gaining the trust and cooperation of at risk populations is especially challenging with HIV because of deep-seated fears about stigma and discrimination that is often associated with having HIV. Moreover, the populations most affected by HIV—gay men, injection drug users, and people of color—all have experienced long histories of oppression, social stigma, and government-sponsored discrimination. These groups enter the HIV arena predisposed to distrust government representatives of any sort—including public health officials.

Also, the most prominent means of transmission of HIV are illegal in many parts of the country. Unauthorized injection drug use is a felony in all fifty states. And anal sex is a crime in twenty-one states and Puerto Rico. Therefore, forcing individuals to identify those with whom they have had risky contact will often constitute a forced admission of criminal activity. . . .

Partner Notification Programs Have Not Worked

As with partner notification for the control of STDs, the effectiveness of partner notification in controlling HIV infection has not been measured in terms of actual reduction in the incidence or prevalence of HIV in any given community. Instead, success in partner notification has largely been defined by the percentage of named contacts that were notified, tested, and found to be HIV positive. But this measure of success ignores substantial evidence that the positive impact of partner notification is limited to a few, specific contexts, and that broad, mandatory implementation is counterproductive from a public health standpoint.

In the first place, mandatory partner notification, whether through requirements aimed at people with HIV or at health care providers, is not enforceable. Many people who participate in partner notification programs simply will not identify partners or will not provide accurate information. For example, a study conducted in North Carolina, where failure of people with HIV to contact their partners is a misdemeanor punishable by a fine, a prison term, or both, found that only 7% of HIV positive people taking part in the study succeeded in notifying their partners. Even after the remaining study participants were given assistance in notifying partners, 66% of identified partners could not be found. In a partner notification program that succeeded in contacting a greater number of named partners, 21% of HIV positive participants still refused to name any partners at all.

In addition, the available evidence does not support the assumption that partners who are notified and tested reduce high-risk behavior or receive effective treatment, thus reducing transmission of HIV. There is growing evidence that perceived risk of exposure to HIV is unrelated to the likelihood that one will take any given preventative action. Instead, it increasingly appears that much more extensive and long-term efforts specifically tailored to the individual needs of those infected with HIV are necessary to change high-risk behavior. In fact, studies that have evaluated behavior change associated with the HIV testing and limited counseling that currently accompanies most partner notification efforts have shown that, unless accompanied by preventive services and intensive counseling, they have little or no effect on changing risk behavior in many high-risk populations.

Why the Effectiveness Is Limited

There are several reasons for the negligible impact of partner notification on rates of HIV infection. One limitation on the effectiveness of partner notification is the fact that there is no medical treatment that renders a person with HIV uninfectious. And what treatments exist are often not available until years after the individual is infected. A recent review of HIV-positive individuals' access to newer and more effective drug therapies demonstrates that a significant number of HIV-positive individuals do not qualify for state AIDS drug assistance programs or Medicaid early in the course of their disease. One medical center in a high-incidence urban area found that the majority of HIV-infected patients tested in the hospital did not even receive adequate referrals for post-discharge care. The sad reality is that many people infected with HIV, especially poor people, are not able to access appropriate medical care. Thus, even if partners are successfully notified, they may not receive the benefit of new drug therapies, or any other treatment for that matter.

Even those with access to treatment face daunting obstacles. Maintaining the rigorous schedule that new drug therapies require can be extraordinarily difficult and successfully reducing risk behavior is a never-ending battle for many. Many new cases of HIV are occurring among people who struggle with homelessness, drug dependency, domestic violence, mental illness, and/or severe poverty. Measures to stabilize peoples' lives so that treatment is successful and to promote lasting behavior change require a commitment of resources far beyond merely notifying someone of their possible exposure to HIV. Services that include readily available treatment for drug dependency and mental illness, housing and job assistance, needle exchange and sustained counseling for risk reduction are necessary to truly diminish the spread of HIV infection. . . .

Partner Notification Is Unsuccessful

Recent proposals to adopt coercive HIV partner notification reject the lessons of decades of public health experience. Public health policy has long emphasized the importance of winning the voluntary cooperation of individuals at risk for exposure to communicable diseases. Moreover, even those partner notification approaches, invoked with increasing frequency in the debate over HIV partner notification, have often failed to stem the spread of sexually transmitted diseases. The reasons for this failure—the inability to locate partners due to the long incubation period of some STDs, the connection between infection and the use of illegal drugs, and the frequency of contact with anonymous partners—are well known features of the HIV epidemic. It is therefore not surprising that the available evidence indicates that coercive partner notification plans have met with little success in campaigns to stem the spread of HIV.

Moreover, coercive partner notification threatens the privacy and civil liberties of people with HIV. Few programs could be more invasive of an individual's right to privacy than programs that require the individual to identify his or her sexual or needle-sharing partners to government agents. Such forced disclosure is made even more troubling by the fact that illegal injection drug use is a felony in all fifty states, and anal sex is a crime in twenty-one states.

Because partner notification violates privacy for no real gain in stemming the AIDS epidemic, the ACLU opposes the adoption of coercive partner notification plans. It is important that people with HIV notify their partners if they may have been exposed to HIV, and the ACLU believes that partner notification services should be part of the standard of care to which every person with HIV is entitled. But partner notification services must be provided on a voluntary, non-coercive, and confidential basis. And, emphasis on partner notification must not become an excuse to divert attention or resources from culturally appropriate, frank education, needle exchange, and other prevention programs that have a proven track record of success.

*"[Nothing] can reduce the transmission of
the virus from mother to infant as
effectively as routine prenatal HIV testing,
with patient notification."*

Voluntary HIV Tests Should Be Routine for Pregnant Women

Marie McCormick

HIV can be transferred from an infected woman to her newborn child. Marie McCormick, chair of the department of
maternal and child health at the Harvard School of Public
Health in Cambridge, Massachusetts, argues that tests for
HIV should be a routine, but not mandatory, part of prenatal care for pregnant women. Women who test positive for
HIV can then be treated with AZT, an anti-AIDS drug that
has been found to substantially prevent the transmission of
HIV from mother to child. McCormick asserts that routine
testing, followed up by counseling if necessary, would do
much to reduce the number of babies born with HIV.

As you read, consider the following questions:
1. When did doctors first learn to prevent the transmission
   of HIV from mothers to their newborns, according to
   McCormick?
2. What reasons does McCormick give for why prenatal
   testing is not routine?
3. What is necessary for routine testing of pregnant women
   for HIV to be effective in reducing HIV transmission?

Marie McCormick, "Prenatal HIV Test Could Save Lives," *North County Times*,
November 7, 1998. Copyright © 1998 by Marie McCormick. Reproduced with
permission.

S ince 1994, doctors have known how to prevent the trans-mission of the AIDS virus from infected mothers to their newborn children. Yet hundreds and possibly thousands of newborns in the United States are infected with the virus each year. Why?

We as a nation have failed to grasp the opportunities made available by our new knowledge. Today the testing of pregnant women for human immunodeficiency virus, or HIV, is still done on a case-by-case basis. As a result, many infected women are not tested and do not receive the care they need.

Maybe their doctors think these women are unlikely to have HIV. Or maybe doctors are too embarrassed to bring up the subject. Many pregnant women still get little if any prenatal care. Far too many HIV infections are missed among these women—with tragic results.

A Way to Solve the Problem

There's a straightforward way of solving the problem, as was pointed out by an Institute of Medicine committee that I chaired. Testing for HIV should become a routine part of prenatal care. Women should be notified that an HIV screen is part of the standard battery of prenatal tests, and given the choice to refuse it. But providing the test as a standard part of prenatal care would lead to far more women being tested.

The 1994 finding that the drug zidovudine, also known as AZT, could substantially reduce the transmission of HIV from mother to infant, was an important success in the fight against AIDS. Thousands of women infected with HIV give birth each year in the United States, and many others who know they are infected consider getting pregnant. This finding revealed to pregnant women the benefits of knowing their HIV status.

A flurry of regulations, policies and guidelines have encouraged pregnant women to be screened. Testing has increased and the number of infected newborns has declined. But the results have not been as good as they should be.

Guidelines typically require health-care providers to give counseling before an HIV test. But many providers see this as a burden and tend not to encourage testing of women they deem unlikely to be infected.

This approach misses many cases of HIV infection. If HIV testing were routine, providers would no longer be making such inherently difficult judgments.

Perinatal HIV Infections Have Declined

During the early 1990s, before perinatal preventive treatments were available, an estimated 1,000–2,000 infants were born with HIV infection each year in the United States. Today, the United States has seen dramatic reductions in mother-to-child, or perinatal, HIV transmission rates. These declines reflect the widespread success of Public Health Service (PHS) recommendations made in 1994 and 1995 for routinely counseling and voluntarily testing pregnant women for HIV, and for offering zidovudine (AZT, also called ZDV) to infected women during pregnancy and delivery, and for the infant after birth.

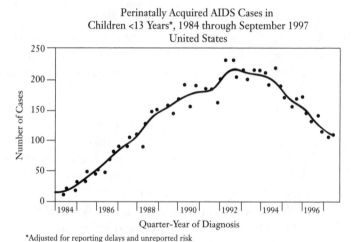

Perinatally Acquired AIDS Cases in
Children <13 Years*, 1984 through September 1997
United States

Quarter-Year of Diagnosis
*Adjusted for reporting delays and unreported risk

Centers for Disease Control and Prevention, "Status of Perinatal HIV Prevention," updated July 24, 1998.

Routine testing with notification would help lessen the stigmatization of particular groups. Testing of all pregnant women would open up new possibilities for education and treatment.

Women should not be forced to be tested. Some women are legitimately concerned about the implications of a positive HIV test. They know it might lead to discrimination, eviction from housing or domestic violence. Doctors need to understand these concerns and work on ways to lessen them.

Treatment Is Also Needed

Routine testing will do little good if HIV-positive women do not have access to high-quality treatment. To be effective, this care should be coordinated through the prenatal, labor, delivery and postnatal periods.

A regional system of prevention and treatment centers, funded by the states and federal government, could help provide this care. The centers could work with primary care physicians to increase awareness of the need for routine testing.

Many other things need to be done to stop AIDS in the United States. Drug-users need access to drug treatment and needle-exchange programs. Young people should learn what they need to protect themselves from infection. More women should receive prenatal care. But none of these steps can reduce the transmission of the virus from mother to infant as effectively as routine prenatal HIV testing, with patient notification.

*"Once mothers are advised of their infants'
HIV status, they can avoid exposing their
children to their own body fluids."*

HIV Testing Should Be Mandatory for Newborns

Wesley J. Smith

Babies who are born with HIV can be successfully treated to prevent or delay the onset of AIDS, asserts Wesley J. Smith in the following viewpoint. Smith argues that HIV tests should be mandatory for all newborns and that mothers should be advised of their child's positive results. Once a mother is told that her infant is HIV-positive, she can begin arranging treatment for her child and take precautions to protect her baby from developing AIDS. Wesley J. Smith is a frequent contributor to the *Weekly Standard* and author of the book *Culture of Death: The Destruction of Medical Ethics in America*.

As you read, consider the following questions:
1. Approximately how many babies are born HIV-positive in New York every year, according to the author?
2. Approximately what percentage of New York babies born HIV-positive actually have AIDS, as cited by Smith?
3. What percentage of HIV-exposed babies have been tested, identified, and given treatment after the passage of the "Baby AIDS" law in New York?

On the face of it, representative Tom Coburn and New York assemblywoman Nettie Mayersohn are mirror opposites: He's a staunch Republican, she's a fiery Democrat; he's pro-life, she's pro-choice; he's socially conservative, she's a booster of gay rights; he's a fundamentalist Christian, she's Jewish; he's Oklahoma, she's pure Queens. But across this yawning political and cultural divide, the two have embraced as allies to promote their common passion—saving newborn babies from AIDS.

Testing Newborns for HIV

A committed feminist who received the New York State National Organization for Women Legislator of the Year Award in 1989, Mayersohn saw praise from the liberal establishment turn to vituperation when she introduced legislation in 1994 requiring HIV testing of all New York newborns and disclosure of the results to mothers of babies who tested positive for the HIV antibody.

It's not as if newborns weren't already being tested. They were—for statistical purposes and to track the course of the epidemic, which revealed that about 1,800 New York State babies were born HIV-positive every year. Between 70 percent and 80 percent of these babies were not actually infected but only tested positive for the antibody. Assuming proper medical treatment and no further exposure to the HIV virus—say, by nursing at their mothers' breasts—most of these babies would not become ill. The other 20 percent to 30 percent actually had AIDS, but quick treatment could extend both the quality and duration of their lives. Unfortunately, strict confidentiality rules enacted at the behest of AIDS activists who fetishize "privacy" meant that mothers could not be informed about their babies' HIV status unless they asked.

Logic, compassion, and a decent regard for the value of these infants' lives (not to mention the lives of the mothers) would seem to dictate public health policies along the lines that Mayersohn proposed. Infected infants should be identified as soon as possible. At that point, they can be treated either to prevent HIV infection or ward off the onset of AIDS. Perhaps more important, once mothers are advised of their infants' HIV status, they can avoid exposing their children to their own body fluids. Unfortunately, logic and true compassion have little to do with much of AIDS public policy.

The fight over Mayersohn's "Baby AIDS" bill was a real donnybrook. Movement feminists, gay activists, ACLU types, some physicians, and legislative colleagues unleashed a near-hysterical hue and cry. Mayersohn became a pariah, turned on angrily by former political allies and friends. "After I introduced the legislation, all hell broke loose," Mayersohn recalls. "On World AIDS Day, I had about 50 activists at my apartment building demonstrating at midnight, going on the intercom demanding to meet. The group's name was Fed Up Queers and they thought that kind of intimidation would be effective in deterring me from doing what I thought was right. They were wrong."

Skewed Priorities

Even more astounding to Mayersohn was the illogic of her opponents' arguments and their skewed priorities: "I was visited by the Gay Men's Health Crisis and they asked me to withdraw the legislation. I said to them, 'Your community has been so devastated by the disease; so many young lives have been lost. Why wouldn't you support this?' And they said, 'Privacy is our main concern.'"

"Then I met with the feminists. I asked them to support my bill. I said, 'This is a woman's bill.' Their response knocked my socks off. They said, 'Well, Nettie, think of the potential for domestic violence the bill will be generating if a guy finds out [his partner's] infected. This is a domestic violence issue.'"

"I said, 'The real violence is getting infected!' If I am in a bad marriage or abusive relationship, I can do something about it. I can get myself out. I can repair a broken jaw. But if someone infects me with HIV, that will mean the end of my life. So, the feminists turned on me. They cared more about politics than fighting disease. I don't understand that kind of mentality." Diane Welsh, president of National Organization for Women (NOW) NYC, typified the response of movement feminists. She denounced Mayersohn's bill as part of "the erosion of a woman's fundamental right to control over her body" and of "a general backlash against women's rights."

Media feminists joined the fray. "What about the mothers?" demanded Anna Quindlen, then a political columnist for the *New York Times*. Rather than support mandatory testing and disclosure, Quindlen proposed, ironically, that pregnant women undergo "mandatory counseling" to induce them to be voluntarily tested. Meanwhile, Richard Gottfried, chairman of the New York Assembly's health committee and an ally of feminists and the AIDS lobby, whined, "If these babies could talk, they'd beg us to protect them by working carefully with their mothers, not by disregarding them."

" FIRST, THE BAD NEWS — IT SEEMS JOE HAD AIDS AND TRANSMITTED IT TO HIS NEWLYWED WIFE AND THEIR NEWBORN CHILD. THE...UM...GOOD NEWS IS THAT JOE'S CIVIL LIBERTIES WEREN'T VIOLATED BY A MANDATORY AIDS TEST. "

Payne. © 1987 by *Scripps Howard*. Reprinted by permission of United Features Syndicate.

The local chapter of NARAL—the National Abortion and Reproductive Rights Action League—had a similar case of the vapors, claiming that testing might "force many women and children out of the health care system entirely." Most appalling, New York NARAL's president called it a "great cause for alarm" that "the interests of newborns were willingly deemed more important than those of women."

Mayersohn fought back. "The real bias," she wrote to the *Village Voice*, "is the failure to even consider that the real discrimination faced by infected individuals is the discrimination against newborns who test positive for the virus at birth.

Unlike children suffering from other diseases for which the state routinely tests at birth, such as syphilis, sickle cell, and hepatitis, children born with the HIV antibody are routinely denied an opportunity to receive treatment because of our strict adherence to a warped definition of confidentiality that says we cannot tell a mother that she is infected and that her child is at risk."

The Tide Is Turning

Slowly, though, the tide turned away from political correctness and toward protecting the lives of newborns exposed to HIV. After a three-year struggle, Mayersohn's legislation passed in June 1996. New York became the first state to require that all newborn infants be tested for HIV and to disclose the results of the testing to the mothers.

Today, the law is working well and saving lives. According to the New York Department of Health, prior to the "Baby AIDS" law about 59 percent of infants with HIV went home from the hospital unidentified to their mothers as having tested positive. By the time of a study published on November 3, 1997, a magnificent 98.8 percent of HIV-exposed infants were being identified and receiving follow-up care.

Mayersohn is thrilled. "With the law, women are coming in," she told me. "They are getting tested; their babies are getting tested. They are not giving birth in the street. They are not jumping off the roof if they are told their babies are HIV-positive. All of these so-called experts and witnesses with alphabet soup after their names who opposed the bill were wrong."

With New York clearly demonstrating that mandatory testing of newborns saves lives without endangering women, the argument should have been settled. But opponents are so steeped in ideology that facts don't matter. So, now it is Coburn's turn to be skewered and roasted over the open flame of vituperation for trying to protect the nation's babies as Mayersohn did New York's.

For five years, Coburn and New York Democrat Gary Ackerman have attempted to pass a New York–style Baby AIDS bill through Congress. They succeeded in 1996, only to have the bill die an ignoble death in a House-Senate conference committee. Frustrated by their inability to break through the AIDS lobby roadblock, they are back in 2000 with a watered down version, the Women's and Children's HIV Protection Act. [The bill died in committee.]

The bill does not require testing. It would merely stiffen the backbones of lawmakers in the 48 states that do not have some form of mandatory testing and identification of infants who test positive for HIV by making those states that fail to pass such laws ineligible for certain AIDS-related federal funding. If Mayersohn could be cloned, the legislation might not be necessary. But given that most legislators are loath to subject themselves to the howling abuse of the AIDS lobby and its allies, a federal courage pill is just what the doctor ordered.

The bill, which would be an amendment to the reauthorization of the Ryan White CARE Act, faces such hysterical opposition that activists threaten to doom Ryan White funding itself rather than permit a federal Baby AIDS bill to become law. Talk about misplaced priorities: These activists would rather see babies die a horrible death in early childhood from AIDS and their states lose desperately needed federal funding than permit the enactment of a public health measure that defies their ideological agenda. "Their belief," says a Coburn aide, "is that if we mandate testing of any segment of society, including infants, we are starting down the path to mandatory testing for everyone."

Mayersohn, a strong supporter of the Coburn/Ackerman legislation, is appalled that AIDS activists seem to have learned nothing from her work: "It is infuriating that AIDS activists are able to thwart national legislation that would promote the kinds of policies that are doing so much good in New York."

Mayersohn is right. The United States is uniquely capable of grappling with the AIDS catastrophe both at home and abroad. But how can we presume to lead the world if we permit ideologues who are blinded by paranoia to thwart the implementation of medical protocols that would do so much to save or improve the lives of AIDS' youngest victims?

Periodical Bibliography

The following articles have been selected to supplement the diverse views presented in this chapter.

Chandler Burr   "The AIDS Exception: Privacy vs. Public Health," *Atlantic Monthly*, June 1997.

Chandler Burr   "Cuba and AIDS," *National Review*, September 29, 1997.

Elizabeth Cross   "Naming Names," *American Medical News*, April 6, 1998.

Liz Galst   "Family Feud," *Poz*, January 1999.

Lawrence O. Gostin and David W. Weffer   "HIV Infection and AIDS in the Public Health and Health Care Systems," *JAMA*, April 8, 1998.

Issues and Controversies on File   "HIV Testing," January 24, 1997.

Theresa M. McGovern   "Is Privacy Now Possible?" *Social Research*, April 2001.

Benjamin F. Neidl   "The Lesser of Two Evils: New York's New HIV/AIDS Partner Notification Law and Why the Right to Privacy Must Yield to Public Health," *St. John's Law Review*, Fall 1999.

Lynda Richardson   "Progress on AIDS Brings Movement for Less Secrecy," *New York Times*, August 21, 1997.

Thomas H. Riess, Kim Christina, and Moher Downing   "Motives for HIV Testing Among Drug Users," *AIDS Education and Prevention*, December 2001.

Cory SerVaas   "Nettie Mayersohn and Her Baby AIDS Bill," *Saturday Evening Post*, January 11, 1998.

Alisa Tang   "Young People Open to HIV Testing," *New York Times*, June 29, 1999.

Laura Ziv   "I Gave Him My Love, He Gave Me HIV," *Cosmopolitan*, February 1998.

CHAPTER 3

How Can the Spread of AIDS Be Controlled?

Chapter Preface

In the mid-1980s, scientists were hopeful that microbicides—chemical compounds that are inserted into a woman's vagina in the form of a gel or suppository—would be effective in killing HIV, the virus widely acknowledged to cause AIDS. Microbicides have killed other sexually transmitted diseases, such as gonorrhea, chlamydia, and herpes, and, it was hoped, they would also kill HIV. Unfortunately, researchers concluded that microbicides did not kill HIV, and in fact, seemed to enable HIV to enter the body more easily.

After studies of microbicides failed to show that they killed HIV, researchers at the University of Texas Medical Branch in Galveston turned their attention to sexual lubricants. The preservatives in the lubricants kill bacteria, so the scientists, led by noted virus researcher Samuel Baron, wondered if the preservatives would kill HIV as well. According to Baron, of the twenty-two lubricants they tested, three killed 99.9 percent of the HIV in infected white blood cells as well as free HIV mixed in with seminal fluid in test tubes. Baron noted that it was not the preservatives that were responsible for killing HIV. He observed, "If they did, all twenty-two lubricants would have worked." They discovered that the three lubricants—Astroglide (also sold under the name Silken Secret), Vagisil, and ViAmor—all contained two common, widely used, and inexpensive compounds that kill HIV. (The researchers refuse to name the compounds until their scientific paper is published sometime in 2002 or 2003.) Baron contends that "[The two compounds] could easily be used by women in Africa and other parts of the world where AIDS is a major problem and where condoms are not popular."

Baron and his fellow researchers may have come up with a new method for reducing the spread of AIDS. Other methods of preventing HIV transmission, such as condoms and needle-exchange programs, are examined by the authors in the following chapter.

*"[Needle exchange programs] can reduce
the number of new HIV infections and do
not appear to lead to increased drug use."*

Needle Exchange Programs Can Control the Spread of AIDS

Peter Lurie and Pamela DeCarlo

HIV is transmitted through blood, thus putting injecting drug users at risk of infection if they share contaminated needles. Peter Lurie and Pamela DeCarlo contend in the following viewpoint that programs that exchange clean needles for used ones—known as needle exchange programs or NEPs—can reduce the spread of HIV/AIDS. Studies show that NEPs do not encourage drug use, and often the programs offer other services to help drug users get off drugs and into treatment. Lurie, a physician and former AIDS researcher at the Center for AIDS Prevention Studies (CAPS), is an assistant professor in the Department of Family and Community Medicine, the Department of Epidemiology and Biostatistics, and the Institute for Health Policy Studies at the University of California in San Francisco. DeCarlo is an AIDS researcher at the CAPS.

As you read, consider the following questions:
1. According to a study cited by the authors, how did HIV infection rates in cities with NEPS compare to rates in cities without needle exchange programs?
2. What steps do the authors recommend to reduce the rate of HIV infection among injecting drug users?

Peter Lurie and Pamela DeCarlo, "Does HIV Needle Exchange Work?" *HIV Prevention Fact Sheet #5 Er*, December 1998. Copyright © 1998 by Center for AIDS Prevention Studies at the University of California. Reproduced with permission.

Why do we need needle exchange? More than a million people in the US inject drugs frequently, at a cost to society in health care, lost productivity, accidents, and crime of more than $50 billion a year. People who inject drugs imperil their own health. If they contract HIV or hepatitis, their needle-sharing partners, sexual partners and offspring may become infected.

It is estimated that half of all new HIV infections in the US are occurring among injection drug users (IDUs). For women, 61% of all AIDS cases are due to injection drug use or sex with partners who inject drugs. Injection drug use is the source of infection for more than half of all children born with HIV.

Injection drug use is also the most common risk factor in persons with hepatitis C infection. Up to 90% of IDUs are estimated to be infected with hepatitis C, which is easily transmitted and can cause chronic liver disease. Hepatitis B is also transmitted via injection drug use.

Needle exchange programs (NEPs) distribute clean needles and safely dispose of used ones for IDUs, and also generally offer a variety of related services, including referrals to drug treatment and HIV counseling and testing.

Sterile Needles Are Not Available

Why do drug users share needles? The overwhelming majority of IDUs are aware of the risk of the transmission of HIV and other diseases if they share contaminated equipment. However, there are not enough needles and syringes available and even these are often not affordable to IDUs.

Getting IDUs into treatment and off drugs would eliminate needle-related HIV transmission. Unfortunately, not all drug injectors are ready or able to quit. Even those who are highly motivated may find few services available. Drug treatment centers frequently have long waiting lists and relapses are common.

Most US states have paraphernalia laws that make it a crime to possess or distribute drug paraphernalia "known to be used to introduce illicit drugs into the body." In addition, ten states and the District of Columbia have laws or regulations that require a prescription to buy a needle and syringe.

Consequently, IDUs often do not carry syringes for fear of police harassment or arrest. Concern with arrest for carrying drug paraphernalia has been associated with sharing syringes and other injection supplies.

In July 1992, the state of Connecticut passed laws permitting the purchase and possession of up to ten syringes without a prescription and making parallel changes in its paraphernalia law. After the new laws went into effect, the sharing of needles among IDUs decreased substantially, and there was a shift from street needle and syringe purchasing to pharmacy purchasing. However, even where over-the-counter sales of syringes are permitted by law, pharmacists are often unwilling to sell to IDUs, emphasizing the need for education and outreach to pharmacists.

What's being done? Around the world and in more than 80 cities in 38 states in the US, NEPs have sprung up to address drug-injection risks. There are currently 113 NEPs in the United States. In Hawaii, the NEP is funded by the state Department of Health. In addition to needle exchange, the program offers a centralized drug treatment referral system and a methadone clinic, as well as a peer-education program to reach IDUs who do not come to the exchange. Rates of HIV among IDUs have dropped from 5% in 1989 to 1.1% in 1994–96. From 1993–96, 74% of NEP clients reported no sharing of needles, and 44% of those who did report sharing reported always cleaning used needles with bleach.

Harm Reduction Central in Hollywood, CA, is a storefront NEP that targets young IDUs aged 24 and under. The program provides needle exchange, arts programming, peer-support groups, HIV testing and case management and is the largest youth NEP in the United States. Over 70% of clients reported no needle-sharing in the last 30 days, and young people who used the NEP on a regular basis were more likely not to share needles.

Needle Exchange and HIV Infection

Does needle exchange reduce the spread of HIV? Encourage drug use? It is possible to significantly limit HIV transmission among IDUs. One study looked at five cities with IDU populations where HIV prevalence had remained low. Glasgow,

Scotland; Lund, Sweden; New South Wales, Australia; Tacoma, WA; and Toronto, Ontario, all had the following prevention components: beginning prevention activities when levels of HIV infection were still low; providing sterile injection equipment including through NEPs; and conducting community outreach to IDUs.

Clean Needles Save Lives

Clean needles save lives. Shared drug needles have caused almost 40 percent of AIDS cases, having infected both drug addicts and their sex partners. Those adults produce 75 percent of the HIV-positive babies. Needle-exchange programs, which Congress forbids the federal government to fund, slash infection rates by allowing addicts to swap used needles for new ones. Such programs, in fact, reduce drug use by steering addicts toward treatment.

Deb Price, *Liberal Opinion Week*, February 15, 1999.

A study of 81 cities around the world compared HIV infection rates among IDUs in cities that had NEPs with cities that did not have NEPs. In the 52 cities without NEPs, HIV infection rates increased by 5.9% per year on average. In the 29 cities with NEPs, HIV infection rates decreased by 5.8% per year. The study concluded that NEPs appear to lead to lower levels of HIV infection among IDUs.

In San Francisco, CA, the effects of an NEP were studied over a five-year period. The NEP did not encourage drug use either by increasing drug use among current IDUs, or by recruiting significant numbers of new or young IDUs. On the contrary, from December 1986 through June 1992, injection frequency among IDUs in the community decreased from 1.9 injections per day to 0.7, and the percentage of new initiates into injection drug use decreased from 3% to 1%.

Hundreds of other studies of NEPs have been conducted, and all have been summarized in a series of eight federally funded reports dating back to 1991. Each of the eight reports has concluded that NEPs can reduce the number of new HIV infections and do not appear to lead to increased drug use among IDUs or in the general community. These were the two criteria that by law had to be met before the federal ban on NEP service funding could be lifted. This is a degree of unanimity on the interpretation of research findings unusual in science. Five of the studies recommended that the federal ban be lifted and two made no recommendations. In the eighth report the Department of Health and Human Services decided that the two criteria had been met, but failed to lift the ban. The Congress has since changed the law, continuing to ban federal funding for NEPs, regardless of whether the criteria are met.

Is needle exchange cost-effective? Yes. The median annual budget for running a program was $169,000 in 1992. Mathematical models based on those data predict that needle exchanges could prevent HIV infections among clients, their sex partners, and offspring at a cost of about $9,400 per infection averted. This is far below the $195,188 lifetime cost of treating an HIV-infected person at present. A national program of NEPs would have saved up to 10,000 lives by 1995.

A Broader Strategy

What must be done? Efforts to increase the availability of sterile needles must be a part of a broader strategy to prevent HIV among IDUs, including expanded access to drug treatment and drug-use prevention efforts. Although the US federal government has acknowledged that NEPs reduce rates of HIV infection and do not increase drug use rates, it still refuses to provide funding for NEPs. Therefore, advocacy activity at the state and local community level is critical. However, the federal government should play a more active role in advocating for NEPs publicly, even if it doesn't fund them.

States with prescription laws should repeal them; those with paraphernalia laws should revise them insofar as they restrict access to needles and syringes. Local governments, Community Planning Groups and public health officials should work with community groups to develop comprehensive approaches to HIV prevention among IDUs and their sexual partners, including NEPs and programs to increase access to sterile syringes through pharmacies.

"*The AIDS virus is spread through voluntary behavior. An unlimited supply of needles will not alter behavior patterns of irresponsible and often psychotic addicts.*"

Needle Exchange Programs Will Not Control the Spread of AIDS

Robert L. Maginnis

Needle exchange programs that allow injecting drug users (IDUs) to swap dirty needles for clean needles do little to slow the spread of AIDS, argues Robert L. Maginnis in the following viewpoint. Maginnis contends that IDUs continue to share needles even when clean needles are available. Maginnis also asserts that discarded needles pose a public health hazard. In addition, the programs send mixed messages about the acceptability of drug use. According to the author, the best solution to protect IDUs from the dangers of HIV/AIDS is treatment. Maginnis is vice president for policy at the Family Research Council, an organization that promotes the traditional family and Judeo-Christian values.

As you read, consider the following questions:
1. What percentage of Americans living with HIV contracted the virus from injecting drug use, according to a report cited by the author?
2. How many states permit needle exchange programs, according to Maginnis?
3. How many needle exchange programs were operating in 1999, according to the North American Syringe Exchange Network?

A cross America there are legal and illegal programs that distribute syringes to drug addicts hoping to slow the spread of the virus that causes AIDS. Even though many of these programs operate in violation of drug paraphernalia laws, they operate under the guise of local health department declarations of "medical emergency." Some governments have even changed pharmacy sales laws to provide ease of access to hypodermic needles. Opposition to these easy access needle programs has been consistent.

Opponents argue that government-sanctioned needle giveaways or changed pharmacy laws that allow virtually unrestricted access to syringes do not slow the spread of AIDS because addicts are unreliable, and that such programs contribute to drug use, not only among current addicts but also among vulnerable adolescents.

Alarmingly, in 1998, the Clinton administration's Secretary of Health and Human Services (HHS) Donna Shalala announced that "a meticulous scientific review has now proven that needle-exchange programs can reduce the transmission of HIV [the virus that causes AIDS] and save lives without losing ground in the battle against illegal drugs."

Barry McCaffrey, then-director of the Office of National Drug Control Policy, publicly disagreed with Shalala's needle decision. "Above all," said McCaffrey, "we have a responsibility to protect our children from ever falling victim to the false allure of drugs. We do this, first and foremost, by making sure that we send them one clear, straightforward message about drugs: They are wrong and they can kill you." McCaffrey's strong views influenced President Bill Clinton not to approve federal AIDS money for needle exchange programs (NEPs).

The Bush administration's National AIDS Policy Coordinator, Scott Evertz, opposes NEPs, believing these programs are not proven to satisfy the law. Hopefully, the new secretary for HHS, Tommy Thompson, will rescind Shalala's NEP decision and Congress will continue to deny funding. . . .

An HIV and AIDS Update

The Center for Disease Control's (CDC) June 2000 HIV/AIDS Surveillance Report found an estimated 500,000 to

600,000 Americans living with HIV and 320,000 people living with AIDS. Among adults living with HIV, a third (33 percent) contracted the virus from homosexual sex and another 15 percent are identified as injecting drug users (IDUs). An additional four percent are identified as having engaged in both behaviors. Patients with HIV identified by heterosexual contact (16 percent) include those who have had sex with drug users, bisexual males, HIV-infected persons and HIV-infected transfusion recipients. The risk factor for nearly a third (30 percent) of all reported HIV cases was not listed or identified in the report.

A majority (53 percent) of AIDS cases have resulted from either male homosexual sex or from male homosexuals who also injected drugs. Another 25 percent were identified as heterosexuals who injected drugs. In these cases, the presumption is that drug-needle sharing is the culprit even though these people may in fact have contracted the virus via sexual contact.

The virus that causes AIDS races through the drug-using population. The surveillance report found that 31 percent of all AIDS cases have been directly or indirectly associated with injecting drug use. That report continues to blame male homosexual sexual contact for 47 percent of all AIDS cases; another six percent of AIDS cases were of gay males who also inject drugs. Forty-one percent of female AIDS patients contracted the virus from injecting drugs, while 40 percent of female AIDS patients contracted it from heterosexual contact exclusively.

Another CDC study found very high rates of HIV infection among young homosexual men. The six-city study conducted between 1998 and 2000 found that 4.4 percent of young homosexual men, twenty-three to twenty-nine years of age, and 14.7 percent of African-American homosexual men in this age group, were infected annually. The HIV incidence was 3.5 percent among Hispanic homosexual men and 2.5 percent among white homosexual men in the study.

A Science Update

Recent science confirms that IDUs share HIV-contaminated equipment even though they have access to an unlimited supply of needles. The following recently published studies

Payne. © 1988 by *Scripps Howard*. Reprinted by permission of United Features Syndicate.

discredit NEP supporters' claims that exchanges limit equipment-sharing.

- A year 2000 article in the *Scandinavian Journal of Infectious Diseases* found that addicts who used an NEP continue to share syringes and other drug-taking paraphernalia like spoons for dissolving the drug. The article cites a London study that found that 65 percent of NEP addicts shared needles with close friends and 20 percent shared equipment with comparative strangers. The study's authors claim that addicts do not consider needle sharing with their steady sex partner to be dangerous.
- A year 2000 article in the *International Journal of Drug Policy* found that addicts commonly share water and filters for preparing injectable substances. Only 10 percent of addicts say they never share water or filters. The study also found that although injectors are aware of the health risks associated with sharing they continue to participate in high-risk sharing activities.
- A 2001 article in the *American Journal of Public Health* found that "any syringe sharing was associated with a three-fold higher risk of Hepatitis C-Virus (HCV) infection. . . . Similarly, risk of HCV was three-fold higher among those who shared a cooker or cotton."

- A 2000 study in the *Journal of Urban Health* found that "there were no significant differences at follow-up between exchange users and non-exchange users in other injection risk practices, such as sharing of drug cookers or filtration cotton or backloading."
- A 2000 National Institute of Drug Abuse study found that addicts are seldom cautious about contamination. The report states,

On only two occasions have we seen members of the network rinse their needles with bleach, despite the fact that we have provided them with bleach sterilization techniques with all of them. All the members of our network visit San Francisco's syringe exchange program and have increased the regularity of clean syringes because of our interaction with them. Nevertheless, it appears that they continue sharing ancillary paraphernalia virtually every single time they inject.

A Legal Update

Federal law prohibits the use of syringes for other than authorized purposes (21 USC § 863). In spite of federal prohibitions, state and local governments have crumbled to needle exchange advocates.

These programs derive from a variety of drug paraphernalia laws across the country. For example, 17 states allow NEPs. Nine states provide exceptions for syringes in their paraphernalia laws. Six states permit nonprescription purchase and possession of syringes and five states require a valid medical prescription for adult purchase or possession of syringes.

The North American Syringe Exchange Network, which promotes exchanges to curb the HIV spread, estimates that as recently as 1999 there were 150 programs operating in 39 states. The exact number is difficult to ascertain because many operate in violation of local paraphernalia laws.

Perhaps the most comprehensive state-by-state survey of operating exchanges is available from the National Conference of State Legislatures' Health Policy Tracking Service. The NCSL's material can be found at www.hpts.org/info/info.nsf.

Society and More Needles

Past FRC [Family Research Council] reports and surveys have demonstrated that citizens are concerned about the hazards created by junkies discarding their dirty needles in public places. That's why most citizens oppose NEPs in their communities.

Citizen fears are not without merit. NEPs distribute millions of syringes every year; accountability is not uniform. That's why some needles end up in places where they create a public hazard. After all, addicts often carelessly discard their syringes, which too often fall into the wrong hands or prick unsuspecting people.

Over the years, FRC has documented examples of the dangers associated with discarded exchange syringes. More examples were found again this year.

- The *Sun Sentinel* reported on February 11, 2001, that a six-year-old from Glade View, Florida, stabbed five children with a discarded syringe.

- The *New York Times* reported on February 2, 2001, that a nine-year-old from the Bronx stabbed four children with a discarded needle.

- The *Frankson & Hastings Independent*, an Australian newspaper, reported on February 13, 2001, that a syringe left at a bus station stuck a four-year-old boy.

Besides the physical hazard created by discarded needles, the fact that NEPs operate in communities has a psychological hazard as well. Previous FRC polls found that most people believe that government-endorsed needle programs send mixed messages to drug-vulnerable people.

What Ought to Be Done?

The AIDS crisis continues, and government has a legitimate role in curbing the spread of the deadly virus. The federal government must not, however, legalize or fund needle giveaway programs until those programs satisfy the strict criteria outlined in the law: that is, the programs are proven to slow the spread of the AIDS virus and do not contribute to more drug use.

Meanwhile, the Bush administration should rescind the Clinton administration's pro-needle decision and then launch an investigation to determine whether the law has been satisfied. Additionally, Congress should direct the General Accounting Office to study the issue to assess the scope of the problem to include whether NEPs are positively impacting the HIV spread and whether there is any evidence that these programs contribute to drug use.

The AIDS virus is spread through voluntary behavior. An unlimited supply of needles will not alter behavior patterns of irresponsible and often psychotic addicts. The best answer for chronic intravenous drug users is abstinence-based and long-term treatment. Unfortunately, for most intravenous drug users, they will not volunteer but must be coerced into treatment.

"Condoms do *protect against [sexually transmitted infections] and HIV, and are most effective when used consistently and correctly."*

Condoms Are Effective at Reducing the Spread of AIDS

Willard Cates Jr.

Willard Cates Jr. is president of Family Health International, an international organization that offers family planning services and information about HIV/AIDS and other sexually transmitted diseases. In the following viewpoint, Cates describes a government report showing that condoms are effective, especially when used consistently and correctly, in preventing most sexually transmitted diseases, including HIV/AIDS. According to Cates, one nation that has definitively shown the effectiveness of condoms is Thailand, where the government implemented an intensive and widespread condom program among prostitutes. The program resulted in a dramatic decrease in the number of new cases of sexually transmitted diseases.

As you read, consider the following questions:
1. What is the most important factor affecting condom failure, according to the report cited by Cates?
2. Why is it not possible to evaluate condom effectiveness using a randomized, controlled trial in which one group does not use condoms, in the author's opinion?
3. How does Thailand provide a real-world example of the condom's effectiveness in controlling the spread of HIV, according to Cates?

Willard Cates Jr., "The NIH Report: The Glass is 90% Full," *Family Planning Perspectives*, September/October 2001. Copyright © 2001 by Alan Guttmacher Institute. Reproduced with permission.

On July 20, 2001, the National Institutes of Health (NIH) released its long-awaited report on condom effectiveness. This report summarized a workshop held more than 13 months previously, in June 2000, to evaluate the scientific evidence on condom effectiveness for preventing sexually transmitted infections (STIs). While both the workshop and the report were generally modeled on the NIH consensus conference approach, the effort had originated as a result of a congressional request, and thus had both a political and a scientific agenda. This tension between politics and science affected not only the origins of this report, but also its processes along the way and its interpretation after it was released.

The Process

Although NIH was responsible for overseeing the workshop and finalizing the report, three other U.S. agencies participated in organizing the review—the Centers for Disease Control and Prevention (CDC), the U.S. Food and Drug Administration (FDA) and the U.S. Agency for International Development (USAID). Each agency brought its own perspective to the table. The NIH provided its focus on molecular and clinical research, the CDC its expertise in epidemiology and prevention, the FDA its interests in product quality and labeling, and USAID its concerns for preventing the spread of STIs and HIV worldwide. The U.S. government representatives formed a Steering Committee for the workshop. In addition, a panel of 28 people was chosen from a spectrum of backgrounds and ideologies to help craft the report. The workshop itself was attended by 180 interested individuals.

The ground rules for the report were made clear from the outset. The panel examined only those peer-reviewed, published articles included in the presentations at the workshop. This limitation ensured that the independent scientific evaluation that occurs prior to publication was inherent in all of the data considered. While this approach allowed a certain quality control, it meant that several bodies of data (e.g., those available but unpublished, or those published but deemed unacceptable by the speakers) were not included in the full set of information considered by the panel. None-theless, an impressive array of 138 peer-reviewed articles that had been published by the time of the workshop were the basis for the NIH report.

The report was limited to evaluating the effectiveness of male latex condoms used during penile-vaginal intercourse. It examined evidence on eight STIs—HIV, gonorrhea, chla-mydia, syphilis, chancroid, trichomoniasis, genital herpes and genital human papillomavirus. The evaluation methodology was extensive, considering both the efficacy (ideal use) and the effectiveness (typical use) of the condom. The quality of the study design, the ascertainment of exposure (e.g., consis-tent condom use), the laboratory measures of outcome (e.g., STIs) and the adequacy of statistical analytic approaches were examined.

The Report

Several main conclusions emerged from the report:

• *Condom quality.* The available male latex condoms are of high quality. Studies based on viral penetration assays have shown condoms to provide a "highly effective barrier to transmission of particles of similar size to those of the small-est [sexually transmitted disease (STD)] viruses."

• *Condom trends.* During the 1980s and 1990s, condom use increased in the United States at the same time that HIV prevention efforts were stepped up. Moreover, the groups in which condom use increased most rapidly are those at great-est risk for STIs—adolescents, young adults and ethnic minorities.

• *Condom failures.* Condom breakage and slippage occurs in an estimated 1.6–3.6% of coital acts. These events are re-lated to user experience with condoms. However, the most important factor affecting condom failure is *nonuse* of the method, rather than breakage or slippage.

• *Condom effectiveness.* Adequate data are available to con-clude that consistent and correct condom use prevents unin-tended pregnancies, HIV infection and gonorrhea in men. Evidence that condom use prevents the other six STIs re-viewed by the panel is insufficient, however.

• *Quality of evidence.* The report emphasized that "the absence of definitive conclusions reflected inadequacies of the evidence available and should not be interpreted as proof of the adequacy or inadequacy of the condom to reduce the risk of STDs other than HIV transmission in men and women and gonorrhea in men." All studies reviewed by the panel were observational in nature and carry a variety of methodological limitations well described in the text.

Unfortunately, as the report states, it is not possible to evaluate condom effectiveness using the ideal study design—a prospective, randomized controlled trial. In populations at high risk for STIs, for ethical reasons individuals cannot be randomized to a group that is not to use condoms. In and of itself, this situation speaks to the acceptance of condom effectiveness as the ethical standard of care within the scientific and clinical communities.

Additional Developments

Between the workshop of June 2000 and the report of July 2001, several events pertinent to its conclusions occurred. In September 2000, CDC convened an expert panel to review its STD Treatment Guidelines. In February 2001, USAID held an open forum to examine the topic of promoting condoms for dual protection against unintended pregnancy and STIs. Finally, on July 5, 2001, responding to the Public Law 106-554 requirement to provide "medically accurate information regarding the effectiveness or lack of effectiveness of condoms in preventing [STDs]," CDC issued a set of "prevention messages" to state health departments and its other grantees. The conclusions of the documents from all three groups were the same—namely, according to H. Gayle, that "correct and consistent use of latex condoms can reduce the risk of [STIs]."

These conclusions were supported both by supplementary data not considered by the panel and by additional literature not covered in the report. For example, four studies not included in the chlamydia section of the report demonstrated that condom use has a protective effect against chlamydia among women; likewise, two studies implied that condoms protected against chlamydia in men. For gonorrhea, a similar situation existed regarding the condom's protective effect among women. Finally, for genital herpes, a recently published study of couples in which one member was infected with herpes simplex virus type 2 and the other was not found that condom use was associated with protection against infection among women. Therefore, this additional scientific literature supports even stronger statements than those contained in the NIH report about the condom's effectiveness against other STIs.

Use Condoms for Protection

I certainly respect the views of the Holy Father and the Catholic Church. In my own judgment, condoms are a way to prevent infection, and therefore I not only support their use, I encourage their use among people who are sexually active and need to protect themselves. I think it's important for young people especially to protect themselves from the possibility of acquiring any sexually transmitted disease, but especially to protect themselves from HIV/AIDS, which is a plague that is upon the face of the earth. . . .

And so I believe condoms are part of the solution to the HIV/AIDS crisis, and I encourage their use by young people who are sexually active. You've got to protect yourself. If you don't protect yourself, who is going to protect you? And you're putting your life at risk when you are having sexual relations with partners who might be infected. And you really don't know whether they are or they are not, do you?

And this is especially the case in sub-Saharan Africa, in the Caribbean, and increasingly a problem in other parts of the world. It was a major American problem and still is. But we have gotten more control over it. But now it is raging out of control in some parts of Africa, Caribbean, elsewhere—China, India—all of these nations will be touched by it, and it is important that the whole international community come together, speak candidly about it, forget about taboos, forget about conservative ideas with respect to what you should tell young people about it. It's the lives of young people that are put at risk by unsafe sex, and therefore protect yourself.

Colin Powell, *An MTV Global Discussion with Colin Powell*, February 14, 2002.

In addition, on August 16, 2001, the United Nations Joint Programme on HIV/AIDS and the World Health Organization issued a statement emphasizing the importance of condoms as "the best defense" in preventing STIs. These organizations underscored the global imperative to continue promoting condoms for HIV prevention. They also worried that contrasting interpretations could detract from efforts to halt HIV spread.

Finally, Thailand provides a real-world example of the condom's effectiveness in stemming the spread of STIs and HIV. In 1991, the Thai government implemented a "100% condom program" to encourage widespread condom use in commercial sex facilities. The proportion of commercial sex acts in which condoms were used increased from a reported 25% in 1989 to 94% in 1995. During the same interval, the incidence of curable STIs reported from government clinics decreased dramatically. Moreover, HIV prevalence among Thai military recruits also decreased.

Thus, whether for individual clinicians counseling clients about their personal risks or for policymakers deciding on the relative value of emphasizing condom use as part of an STI and HIV prevention strategy, the data are compelling: Condoms *do* protect against STIs and HIV, and are most effective when used consistently and correctly.

The Interpretations

The response to the report was immediate and polarized. A group of physicians held a press conference to proclaim that the report demonstrated the ineffectiveness of condom use. These advocates, including former Congressman Tom Coburn, saw themselves as exposing the "fact that condoms are ineffective in preventing transmission of most STDs, thus challenging the notion of 'safe sex' as championed by the CDC." Unfortunately, by inferring that absence of data meant condom ineffectiveness, the group did exactly what the report cautioned readers not to do. The group went even further in calling for the resignation of CDC director Jeffrey Koplan, alleging that his agency had "deliberately misrepresented condom effectiveness." Moreover, they implied the only reason the report had been released was that they had filed a Freedom of Information Act request.

On the other side, some congressional representatives criticized the report for its "misleading statements regarding the effectiveness of condoms." These politicians felt that the report understated the strong epidemiologic evidence supporting the effectiveness of condoms against such infections as chlamydia, gonorrhea, trichomoniasis and genital herpes. Stating that the report was flawed and undermined public confidence in condoms, they feared that this could lead to "decreases in condom use and increases in risky behavior, and the spread of [STIs]." The representatives called for an independent review of the scientific evidence by the Institute of Medicine.

Even press headlines reflected the dichotomy of opinion. CNN, the first news service to break the report, proclaimed "Condom report questions STD protection" on its website. However, the Associated Press declared, "Condoms protect against HIV, gonorrhea." A variety of follow-up articles expressed clinicians' concern about the report's being misinterpreted, although both sides had generated their own spin.

The Take-Home Messages

First, the report itself was a quality effort. The NIH and the other federal agencies did their assigned job by reviewing and summarizing the available scientific evidence. The main problem was timeliness, caused in part by multiple reviews to accommodate sensitivities to political misinterpretation.

Second, from a public health perspective, the data clearly show that the glass is 90% full (that condoms are relatively effective) and only 10% empty (that data are inadequate). Male condom mechanics and quality assurance are good; moreover, levels of condom breakage and slippage are low and are not a major public health problem. At both the individual and the population levels, nonuse of male condoms is the predominant factor affecting condom failure. Because trends in condom use among the highest-risk populations have been encouraging, interpretations of the data that would discourage condom use might enhance the spread of STIs.

Third, existing studies demonstrate that the effectiveness of male condoms varies by the particular STI. In part, this is what I call the condom's "forgiveness factor"—namely, its ability to withstand certain levels of inconsistent use without allowing transmission of an infection (or permitting a pregnancy). This forgiveness measure is directly related to the organism's "beta"—its ability to be transmitted during a single act of unprotected intercourse. In general, the lower the beta, the higher the forgiveness with imperfect use. HIV is less easily transmitted and gonorrhea is more easily transmitted during unprotected coitus; thus, the condom is more forgiving of imperfect use when it comes to HIV prevention than it is for gonorrhea prevention.

Fourth, the inadequacy of the data should not be interpreted as indicating the inadequacy of condoms. Deliberate attempts to characterize the evidence as demonstrating the "ineffectiveness of condoms" constitute a misunderstanding of what the report states. Moreover, such misrepresentation can undermine the public's confidence in condoms, thereby leading to nonuse and to further spread of STIs and HIV.

The Next Steps

The data presented in the report, as well as subsequent evidence available since the workshop, are clear. Male latex condoms are effective in preventing the most serious STI (HIV), the most easily transmitted STIs (gonorrhea and chlamydia) and another important sexually transmitted condition (unplanned pregnancy). A crucial qualifier to this statement is that condoms work best when they are used consistently and correctly. All public health messages must reinforce the notion of condom effectiveness. The goal is to increase levels of consistent and correct male condom use in sexually active populations with a high prevalence of STIs and HIV.

Having emphasized that condoms work, we must also realize they do not work perfectly. But nothing in medicine (or in life, for that matter) always works. A full decade before the hoopla generated by this report, absolutist approaches to HIV prevention were being demanded: In 1991, an article in a national periodical was entitled "There is no safe sex." The author argued that because condoms were not foolproof in preventing HIV infection, the combination of abstaining from sex until marriage and practicing monogamy thereafter provided our only hope against the further spread of HIV. This is the same recommendation being made today by the physician advocacy group.

We must not, in Voltaire's terms, let "the best be the enemy of the good." Our prevention approaches—not only to

HIV, but to other conditions as well—recognize that incremental, partially effective steps are necessary to mount collectively effective (but imperfect) prevention programs. The aggregation of these combination prevention strategies can have a dramatic effect on HIV spread.

The STI and HIV epidemics are not monolithic events that happen in the same way or at the same rate in all groups. They are not uniformly susceptible to claims of panacea-prone advocates. Controlling the spread of STIs will require different, mutually reinforcing techniques to reach the myriad of groups in our pluralistic society. The NIH condom report shows that male latex condoms are effective interventions that help to prevent the spread of STIs and unintended pregnancy. They must be the mainstay of our dual protection strategies both in the United States and globally. Any attempt to undermine their use will have a negative and long-lasting public health impact.

4

*"The condom is not fool-proof protection
either against pregnancy or HIV."*

Condoms Do Not Protect Against HIV

Orestes Monzon

Thailand has often been applauded for the effectiveness of its condom program in controlling the spread of AIDS. In the following viewpoint, Orestes Monzon maintains that condoms, and the Thai condom program, do not provide adequate protection against HIV or pregnancy. The AIDS virus is much smaller than sperm, he asserts, and therefore it is able to easily pass through the microscopic pores in condoms. In addition, condoms are frequently handled improperly, thus increasing the chances they will break or tear, which can reduce their effectiveness. According to Monzon, urging children to use condoms condones casual sex. He states that the most effective protection against HIV and pregnancy is abstinence. Monzon, the executive director of Human Life International, is secretary general of the Association of Southeast Asian Nations' Association of Radiology.

As you read, consider the following questions:
1. How many Thais were projected to be infected with HIV by 2000, according to the author?
2. What is the failure rate of condoms, as cited by Monzon?
3. In the author's view, what are some of the ways in which condoms can be improperly handled?

Orestes Monzon, "The Great Thailand Experiment: Why Condoms Shouldn't Be Used to Fight AIDS," *HLI Reports*, January 1997. Copyright © 1997 by Human Life International. Reproduced with permission.

A recent meeting of the ASEAN (Association of Southeast Asian Nations) task force on AIDS noted the continued opposition of the region's conservative societies and resolved to promote more aggressively the use of condoms to stem the disease. It held up Thailand's efforts to promote the condom as a model for the rest of the region. "Everyone looks at what happened to Thailand," Reuter quoted an Indonesian official as saying. "They have a lot to share with us."

Presumably, the Philippine government, which has increasingly ignored the religious and cultural sensibilities of Filipinos by advocating the use of condoms and even by having some public school students instructed on how to use them, shares the view that Thailand is the best model to fight AIDS.

But is it really? Alas, no. Thailand is the region's worst AIDS case, with more than one million Thais projected to be infected with the HIV virus by the year 2000. Thailand's number-one fan, Indonesia, has the next worst case with around 750,000 cases by the end of the 1990s, followed by Vietnam with 300,000 cases. "Conservative" societies like the Philippines and Malaysia will have 90,000 and 30,000 cases, respectively.

For medical practitioners like me, the trumpeting of Thailand as the region's best AIDS-prevention performer is insane.

Widespread Condom Promotion

Thailand was ahead of the region in starting widespread condom promotion. As early as the 1970s, it had been distributing condoms to prostitutes, their clients, and just about everyone—including children with no knowledge of the sexual act. The popular Thai health minister earned the sobriquet "Mr. Condom" for his creative ways of promoting the "rubber" by demystifying it. Many of us still remember him blowing a condom and popping it like a balloon during a talk at the Asian Institute of Management. He even got a Magsaysay Award for his campaign.

But all the awards given him and the praises heaped on him by an adulatory media won't sugar-coat the fact that Thailand is losing the battle against AIDS. Thousands are dying in Thailand because of an irresponsible campaign that views illicit sex as alright just as long as it is "safe." Thousands of Filipinos will die too if the government persists in its "safe-sex" campaign.

The reason is simple. The condom is not fool-proof protection either against pregnancy or HIV. It has a failure rate of 12 to 18 percent in preventing pregnancy. Some studies even show a failure rate of up to 30 percent.

HIV: Smaller than Sperm

Presumably the failure rate for AIDS prevention is higher because HIV is much smaller than sperm. This fact was driven home during the uproar in 1992 when the Washington, D.C. government passed out condoms in the public schools in a campaign to make "sexual relations with HIV carriers safe."

C.M. Roland, head of the Polymer Properties Section of the Naval Research Laboratory on rubber, chemistry and technology, criticized the move. "Because the AIDS virus is in order of magnitude smaller than the sperm, the situation is actually worse," he said, explaining that the virus is only 0.1 micron in size.

Roland added: "Moreover, there exists direct evidence of voids in rubber-comprising condoms. Electron micrographs reveal voids of 5 microns in size (50 times larger than the virus), while fracture mechanics analyses, sensitive to the largest flaws present, suggest inherent flaws as large as 50 microns (500 times the size of the virus)."

Another reason why the condom fails is improper handling. Latex condoms can be damaged through exposure to air pollution, heat and light, ozone and humidity. In the sexual act itself, condom slippage and breakage rates are as high as 15 percent.

Ingredient for Disaster

Many condom advocates, in and out of government, are now urging that children be educated in the use of condoms. In fact, there are reports that students in some public schools in Manila and Cebu are taking part in pilot projects by the education department to promote condom use. This is a sure ingredient for disaster, partly because it rests on the thin hope that young people will use condoms reliably.

Parents may well wonder whether children who sometimes forget closing the door behind them can ever remember to use a condom while in the heat of passion. And if they do, can they use it correctly?

SAFER NOW?

Locher. © 1991 by *Chicago Tribune*. Reprinted with permission.

Even the most "modern" of societies with long experience in contraception aren't exemplary in the proper use of condoms. Witness the United States, where leaders of value-free sex education and promotion of contraception and abortion among her young people have not exactly brought about a decreased incidence of teenage pregnancies, much less a decline in AIDS cases. For that matter, witness Thailand.

What seems to have been overlooked by our health planners is that massive condom promotion in Thailand goes hand-in-hand with the massive sex tourism which has underpinned that country's fantastic growth since the 1970s. Uncritical Filipinos always marvel at the Thais for not having any "hang-ups" about casual sex and point to their Buddhist religion—presumably open-minded, as contrasted with "medieval" Catholicism—as the cause. But as shown by the Thai government's aggressive promotion of condoms and prostitution, the reason is not cultural or religious, but commercial.

Kid-Glove Treatment of Prostitution

Considering our government's kid-glove treatment of prostitution, we may not be too far behind Thailand. In fact, health workers are reputed to be working double-time to distribute condoms to prostitutes. Moreover, red-light districts have sprouted in Manila and Cebu, the prostitution dens operating with protection from corrupt police and local officers. These places are even built near schools without the authorities raising a finger.

Now, even the schools are slowly becoming part of the sex industry. With the gradual introduction of amoral sex-education modules that instruct children in the use of condoms and other contraceptives, with the bombardment of young people with "safe-sex" messages in the media, the government is condoning casual sex and (indirectly) mercantile prostitution.

Instead of teaching the young the right values and the proper regard for the sexual act, our government is using the schools and the media to cheapen sex. The beneficiary of all this is sex tourism. We don't know if this is part of the Ramos administration's "moral recovery program."

Thus, it behooves parents to establish their own "moral recovery program." They should not allow their children to fall prey to the government's "safe-sex" promotion, which is a mask for its alliance with white slavery.

The condom and other contraceptives are protection neither against "unwanted" pregnancy nor AIDS. The most effective protection is chastity, the proper regard for the sexual act, which only practicing Christian parents can teach their children. Good parents know that sex is neither "safe" nor "unsafe." It is either moral or immoral.

"Vaccines are the most cost-effective medical intervention of all time, the only way any disease has ever been eradicated."

An AIDS Vaccine Is Needed to End the Epidemic

Bill Snow

Bill Snow, the editor of the *HIV Vaccine Handbook*, is an active member of several HIV/AIDS research committees and organizations. In the following viewpoint, Snow argues that the best way to cure AIDS is to prevent it in the first place. Since in the past, vaccines were used to prevent people from getting diseases, he contends that HIV vaccines must be developed to prevent AIDS. A vaccine against AIDS is possible, he asserts, and more research should be devoted to developing one.

As you read, consider the following questions:

1. What percentage of new infections are found in the developing world, according to Snow?
2. Why are methods of prevention like condoms and needle exchange not enough to fight AIDS, in the author's opinion?
3. In Snow's view, what factors are extremely important in order for an HIV vaccine to be developed?

The questions are seldom voiced. Reporters are the only ones who ever asked me outright, but friends have occasionally made disparaging asides, in private. Those in the know—the treatment activists—have been extraordinarily supportive.

Why would someone with AIDS put so much energy into the search for a preventive vaccine? Won't money and attention be taken away from treatments and care? What will happen to *us* when *they* get a vaccine?

My answers are complex, and there are risks to avoid; your conclusions and choices may be different, but I hope we all end up in the same place on this one.

Looking Back

I've been infected for 15 years. Looking back, I remember my acute viral syndrome, but of course we didn't know what it was at the time. I was on my first visit to Venice, with my new lover. We figured I'd gotten sick on some black risotto or had the German measles. The Italian doctor we called in didn't have a clue. . . .

As many of you know, 15 years is a very long time to live with fear, fear of infection, fear of illness, and fear of death. After a while, one gets to know one's fears and gets a little bored with them.

I've tested positive for nine years. When I found out, I'd been with that same lover for six years and we thought we'd been safe long enough. My life was suddenly split into two, before and after. I joined ACT UP [a gay activist organization], read newsletters, and had dozens of T cell counts; I tried to follow the advice of Project Inform ("it's never too early") and looked for something to do.

I first heard about HIV vaccines the next year. Jonas Salk, a culture hero from my childhood, proposed that still healthy immune systems could be stimulated to fight off the virus better and longer with therapeutic vaccines. So for purely selfish reasons, I took this up, joined a trial, and started to be seduced by the potential—and the drama—of HIV vaccines. Therapeutic vaccines don't seem to add much to the ongoing battle between the immune system and the virus, but preventive vaccines may tip the balance by preparing the immune system before it sees HIV. (My trial and all the other therapeutic vaccine trials so far have had no measurable effect on T cells, viral load, or any clinical aspects of HIV infection.)

The logic is irrefutable and a cliché: an ounce of prevention is worth a pound of cure. Nine-tenths of new infections are in the developing world with no resources for treatments. Vaccines are the most cost-effective medical intervention of all time, the only way any disease has ever been eradicated, and—if you don't already know, take my word for it—treatment is imperfect, expensive, and very difficult to live with.

We Can End the AIDS for All Time

The scientific consensus is that an AIDS vaccine is possible. Non-human primates have been protected by experimental AIDS vaccines. Some people repeatedly exposed to HIV resist infection and mount HIV specific immune responses, providing important clues for the design of an effective AIDS vaccine. Other infectious diseases have been controlled by vaccines. Smallpox was eradicated in 1977 because of an effective vaccine. Polio has been eliminated in the Americas and projections are that it will be eliminated globally by the end of 2005. Measles and yellow fever have been controlled by vaccines.

The prospects for success have never been greater.

Advances in molecular biology and basic HIV research have led to the development of promising strategies for effective AIDS vaccines.

International AIDS Vaccine Initiative, "The World Needs an AIDS Vaccine," 2002.

I've been on antivirals for seven years. I've taken eight of them, singly, in pairs, triple therapy, and now fours—pickling myself from the inside out. At last count I had 15 mutations in my protease gene and 16 in my reverse transcriptase, so I'm running out of backups. I'm not as young anymore either. It's too late to die young, and I have the guilty pleasure of living on borrowed time.

The emotions are the problem. Actually emotion, singular—fear. Old fears: fear of sickness, fear of pain, fear of death, fear of abandonment, free-floating fear; and new fears: fear of making the wrong treatment decision, fear of missing out on the new drug, fear of having the worst side effects.

But no matter what your sero- or social status, we all have our own problems and we have our common problems. Humankind has a problem: a virus. Its little enzyme scissors are chopping us up: dead-alive, sick-well, uninfected-undetectable-treatment failures, insured-uninsured, rich-poor. It has infected our lives.

I don't know how anyone can live with this disease for even a day and wish it on their worst enemies.

I also feel an incredibly close connection with people who have this disease, who fear and avoid it, and who fight it. That's what got me hooked into the preventive vaccine effort. Eight years ago, virtually no one was paying attention, and it took that long for the International AIDS Conferences and the G-8 countries, the president and Congress, even the National Institutes of Health to catch on.

Survival and Mortality

So why not push for a vaccine? Survival is not the issue. Mortality is a problem everyone has to face. We've just been forced to do it more insistently and at a younger age. I don't know about you, but that's done me some good. We've all seen it happen: the sicker you get, or the more afraid, the smaller your world becomes until you're alone and darkness closes in. I for one would like to delay going there.

I now know more uninfected than infected people. The ones who are newly infected live in a different world from me. They don't know when or if they'll ever get sick. They don't have an easy time finding a partner; I still live with mine.

A lot can and should be done for prevention now—safer sex, condoms, needle exchange, and the like—but if you know anything about human nature, you know we can never change behavior enough. We need a vaccine in the prevention mix, and we need it as soon as we can make it happen. Many researchers agree that a vaccine is possible. Given the potential, there is simply not enough attention and not enough activity for HIV vaccines. Progress is slow, and we don't know when we'll get what we want. Public pressure and commitment to develop a vaccine are extremely important. Ten years of AIDS advocacy has shown us that the spotlight makes things happen.

So, let's answer the original questions:

Why would someone with AIDS put so much energy into the search for a preventive vaccine?

Fascination, great people, the thrill of the chase. Enormous respect for treatment activists who are doing a great job without me. Sheer perversity.

Won't money and attention be taken away from treatments and care?

Not if we fight that together.

What will happen to us when we get a vaccine?

The world will be a much better, safer place. To be totally honest, we *all* may be long gone, infected or not. Is that any reason to hold back?

"Why embark on a huge national venture to create a vaccine for a disease that is already extraordinarily preventable?"

An AIDS Vaccine Is Not Needed to End the Epidemic

Charles Krauthammer

Charles Krauthammer is a syndicated columnist. In the following viewpoint, Krauthammer argues that developing a vaccine for HIV/AIDS is a waste of time and money. He asserts that the disease is easily preventable because it is not acquired through casual contact but through avoidable behaviors such as unprotected sex and injection drug use. HIV/AIDS can be controlled by better public health efforts to reduce these dangerous behaviors instead of wasting money and time on developing a vaccine for a preventable disease.

As you read, consider the following questions:
1. According to the author, when did President Clinton pledge the United States would have an AIDS vaccine?
2. On what should the country's intellectual, scientific, and financial resources be spent, if not for an AIDS vaccine, in Krauthammer's opinion?
3. What public health measures should be applied to AIDS, in Krauthammer's view?

The reviews are in on President Bill Clinton's dramatic declaration on May 18, 1997, pledging the United States to finding an AIDS vaccine, moonshot-like, within 10 years. Apart from AIDS activists who complain that the president did not commit serious moonshot money to the enterprise ("cheap talk"—playwright Larry Kramer), the reaction was mostly favorable. Who, after all, can be against a vaccine against anything?

No one seems to want to raise the obvious, if indelicate, question: Why embark on a huge national venture to create a vaccine for a disease that is already extraordinarily preventable?

A Preventable Disease

Unlike most communicable diseases, AIDS is not contracted casually. Unlike tuberculosis, it is not contracted by being coughed on in the subway. Unlike dysentery, it is not contracted by drinking the wrong water. To get AIDS you must, in all but the rarest cases, engage in complex consensual social behavior, namely unsafe sex or intravenous drug abuse.

It would be nice to live in a world where one could engage in such behaviors while enjoying vaccine-induced immunity. But is that really a top national priority? Would any president propose as a top national priority an anti-lung-cancer vaccine so that people who smoke—48 million Americans do—could do so with immunity?

Nor do presidents call for a 10-year campaign to produce a vaccine against cirrhosis of the liver. Why? Not because we want to stigmatize people who drink or smoke. But for a very practical reason: These behaviors being voluntary and preventable, it makes a lot more sense to spend the scarce intellectual, scientific and financial resources of the country trying to give people immunity from diseases that they cannot otherwise protect themselves against.

The classic case is polio. When Franklin D. Roosevelt contracted it in 1921, we had not a clue how people got it. By the 1950s, frightened parents kept their children away from swimming pools and movie theaters and even crowds. They lived in terror not knowing what they might be doing that was contributing to their kids' chances of getting polio.

143

With no obvious behavioral cause, polio was the classic case of a disease crying out for a vaccine. Meningitis, cervical cancer and multiple sclerosis occupy a similar position today. But AIDS?

A Tricky Little Vaccine

All the trumpeting we hear about an "AIDS vaccine" raises more questions. For example, if HIV is really "always mutating," what will the development costs be for the continual updating of a "tricky little vaccine" to mutate right along with it?

More troubling is the fact that, prior to the AIDS era, it was commonly accepted that the purpose of a vaccine was to stimulate the immune system into responding to a faux virus by manufacturing antibodies. In fact, antibody tests are commonly used to determine if a vaccine has been effective, and to make judgements about whether a booster shot is needed.

In response to the idea of the vaccine, along with other skeptics, I have pointed to another paradox: if the AIDS industry is going to market a "vaccine," how are they to determine its effectiveness in preventing disease, except by testing for the very same HIV antibodies always claimed earlier to confirm active and threatening presence of the alleged lethal agent?

Michael Wright, "The Contradictions and Paradoxes of AIDS Orthodoxy," July 2000.

Moreover, Clinton is calling for a huge technological innovation (which many in the field doubt is a reasonable prospect anyway) to prevent the spread of AIDS. Yet, at the same time, the traditional way of controlling the spread of communicable diseases has been largely abandoned in the case of AIDS. And uniquely in the case of AIDS.

Traditional Methods of Prevention Abandoned

We fight just about every epidemic—tuberculosis, syphilis, gonorrhea—by identifying carriers and warning their contacts. The usual epidemiological tracing has not been done for AIDS. Gay activists and civil libertarians have vociferously opposed it. And the politicians have caved.

The story of this travesty—"the effective suspension of traditional public health procedures for AIDS"—is laid out in damning detail by Chandler Burr in the June 1997 *Atlantic Monthly* ("The Aids Exception: Privacy vs. Public Health"). "AIDS has been so thoroughly exempted from traditional public health approaches," writes Burr, "that civil libertarians have defeated in court attempts by health authorities to notify the spouses of people who have died of AIDS that their husbands or wives were HIV-infected."

In 1985, in fact, gay activists brought suit to prevent use of the first test for HIV, unless assured the tests would not be used for widespread screening of gays. Even today they oppose the mandatory HIV screening of pregnant women, even though we know that early treatment of the mothers would reduce by 50 to 75 percent the number of kids born with HIV.

No Routine Screenings or Tests

"Traditional public health is absolutely effective at controlling infectious disease," says Dr. Lee Reichman, who works with tuberculosis and AIDS patients. "It should have been applied to AIDS from the start, and it wasn't. Long before there was AIDS, there were other sexually transmitted diseases [STDs], and you had partner notification and testing and reporting. This was routine public health at its finest and this is the way STDs were controlled."

Marcia Angell, executive editor of the *New England Journal of Medicine*, is blunter than most: "I have no doubt . . . that if, for example, we screened all expectant mothers, we could prevent AIDS in many cases. And if we traced partners, we would prevent AIDS in many cases. And if we routinely tested in hospitals, we would prevent AIDS in many cases."

And if we had a president with guts, he would be demanding these elementary measures to save people from getting AIDS today—instead of waving a wand and telling scientists to produce for him a magic vaccine 10 years from now.

"Comprehensive sexuality education that advocates abstinence yet provides education . . . has proven practical and effective [in reducing AIDS]."

Sex Education That Includes Abstinence Will Reduce the Spread of AIDS

AIDS Action

AIDS Action is an organization committed to advocating for people affected by HIV/AIDS. In the following viewpoint, the organization maintains that sex education programs need to combine abstinence with comprehensive sex education. Programs that include both abstinence and comprehensive sex education are effective at protecting teens from contracting HIV/AIDS and do not result in an increase of sexual activity or early initiation of sex. Abstinence education encourages teens to refrain from sex, while comprehensive education gives them the knowledge they need to protect themselves against HIV/AIDS should they become sexually active. Studies have found that this type of education program delays the onset of sexual intercourse and reduces the frequency of intercourse and the number of sexual partners.

As you read, consider the following questions:

1. What percentage of HIV infections occur in people under age twenty-five, as cited by the author?
2. What were the results of a survey of girls who regularly discussed sex with their parents, according to AIDS Action?

AIDS Action, "Abstinence Education and HIV/AIDS," *AIDS Action Policy Facts*, August 2001. Copyright © 2001 by AIDS Action. Reproduced with permission.

Each year, half of all new HIV infections in the United States are among individuals under age 25. Two young Americans under the age of 25 are infected with HIV every hour, resulting in 20,000 new infections per year among young people. Yet federal funding trends support abstinence-only education rather than comprehensive abstinence and sexual health education programs that prepare teenagers for the world outside their classrooms. By graduation, 65 percent of all high school seniors report having had sex. Full knowledge of the options available to adolescents, from abstinence to safer sex, is important in empowering young people, influencing the choices they make about sex, and preventing new HIV infections. Abstinence-only programs do not meet the needs of America's youth in their quest for the information and skills necessary to make good decisions and stay healthy.

While abstinence-only programs focus exclusively on abstaining from sexual activity until marriage, abstinence-plus programs seek to educate individuals about all facets of sexual health with a focus on abstinence. Information regarding the prevention of sexually transmitted diseases (STDs), including HIV, is discussed in addition to highlighting the option of abstaining from sexual activity until marriage. Research has shown that comprehensive sex education programs that discuss both abstinence and protection from sexually transmitted diseases actually delay the onset of sexual intercourse, reduce the frequency of intercourse, and reduce the number of sexual partners.

Abstinence-Plus Education Works

Comprehensive sexuality education that advocates abstinence yet provides education for those teens that choose to become sexually active has proven practical and effective. Abstinence-plus education, which provides a range of information and options for young people from abstinence to safer sexual behavior, does not increase sexual activity or lower the age of a young person's first sexual encounter. There is no evidence that abstinence-only education is effective in preventing or delaying sexual activity. In fact, a recent abstinence-only initiative in California actually resulted in more students reporting sexual activity after participating in the program.

Concerns that discussing explicit sexual information with youth would result in an increase in sexual activity or early initiation of sex among youth have proven unfounded. A recent Institute of Medicine (IOM) report supported abstinence-plus programs, citing studies that found that teens with comprehensive sexuality education were less likely to engage in sexual intercourse, and those who had sex did so less often and were more apt to use protection.

Surveys have shown that an overwhelming majority of parents want their children to receive information about sex, including both abstinence and contraception, from trained professionals at schools. Parents who engage their children in frank discussions of STD and HIV risk are quite effective: A study of mother-adolescent communication regarding HIV demonstrated an increase in condom use only for teens whose mothers had talked to them about condoms before they became sexually active. Similarly, a survey of 522 African-American adolescent girls found that those girls who regularly discussed sex with their parents were significantly less likely to engage in behavior that placed them at risk for HIV and much more likely to bring up STD/HIV prevention with sexual partners than girls whose parents did not discuss sex, STDs, and HIV.

Current Trends and Programs

Comprehensive sexuality education helps to minimize behavior that places adolescents at risk for HIV, and it is in demand among American youth. Most teens know about HIV transmission, but they want to know more about protecting themselves against HIV. Today's teens need information about sexual behavior and HIV/AIDS. The Kaiser Family Foundation has found that 68 percent of all sexually active teens did not think they were personally at risk of contracting HIV. However, 65 percent of sexually active teens are personally concerned about HIV/AIDS.

According to the IOM and the Presidential Advisory Council on HIV/AIDS, a significant challenge in preventing HIV transmission among teens is the increasing number of abstinence-only sex education programs in schools. These programs are offered in place of comprehensive or abstinence-plus sex education programs. Additionally, in his recent *Call to Action*, Surgeon General David Satcher asserted, "given that one-half of adolescents in the United States are already sexually active—and at risk of unintended pregnancy and STD/HIV infection—it also seems clear that adolescents need accurate information about contraceptive methods so that they can reduce those risks." There is no evidence to support the widespread adoption of abstinence-only programs, whereas providing teens with more information has been found to delay the initiation of sexual activity and promote better overall health.

In 1991, most (35) states require sexuality education to be taught in school. In eleven of those states, the curriculum must focus on abstinence until marriage, with brief mention of STD and HIV prevention. In two of those states, HIV prevention education is only discussed in the context of abstinence until marriage. In three of the states that do not require sexuality education, if it is taught voluntarily, the program can only discuss abstinence until marriage. The number of states requiring abstinence-only education is growing. In 1988, two percent of public school teachers reported teaching abstinence as the sole method of protection against sexually transmitted diseases (STDs) including HIV. That number rose to 23 percent by 1999.

There is a growing trend of providing abstinence-only education at the expense of comprehensive sexual education that includes abstinence as well as pregnancy, STD, and HIV prevention. Abstinence-plus programs provide teenagers with a range of options and information. With half of all new HIV infections in the U.S. each year occurring among teens and young adults, more information about HIV prevention could prevent additional infections. Abstinence-only programs do not provide young people with the information or negotiation skills that they may need to protect themselves from HIV infection.

| *"HIV prevention works—and at a fraction of the cost of drug treatment."*

Prevention Is the Best Way to Control the Spread of AIDS

Peter Lamptey and Willard Cates Jr.

Peter Lamptey and Willard Cates Jr. argue in the following viewpoint that the best way to address the HIV/AIDS epidemic is to prevent the infection from occurring in the first place. There is no cure for AIDS, and the drug cocktails used to treat AIDS are not effective for everybody. The authors assert that programs that stress changes in behavior to avoid infection are fundamental to reducing the spread of AIDS. Moreover, it is much less costly to prevent HIV/AIDS than it is to treat the disease. Lamptey is president of the Family Health International AIDS Institute (FHI) and directs FHI's AIDS Control and Prevention project. Cates is president and chief executive officer of FHI and oversees the HIV/Network for Efficacy Trials for the National Institutes of Health.

As you read, consider the following questions:

1. According to the authors, how much does drug treatment cost per year?
2. What circumstances could cause HIV to mutate, as cited by Lamptey and Cates?
3. In the authors' opinion, why will prevention programs still be necessary when a vaccine for HIV/AIDS is found?

Since the XIth International AIDS Conference in Vancouver in 1996, news of continued important treatment breakthroughs has raised hopes and expectations. Researchers have reported that the new protease inhibitors, taken in combination with other AIDS drugs such as AZT, ddC and 3TC, can reduce the amount of HIV in infected people to undetectable levels. Some scientists even speak—cautiously—about the possibility of eradicating HIV from infected people. As testimony to the optimism, the popular U.S. magazine *Time* proclaimed Dr. David Da-i Ho of Aaron Diamond Research Institute in New York as its 1996 "Man of the Year" for his scientific leadership in these treatment efforts.

The results from trials of a new generation of anti-HIV drugs are indeed encouraging. But the excitement over these findings has obscured what is—and will continue to be—our most potent weapon against the virus: prevention. Worse still, it may undermine prevention efforts by encouraging the mistaken impression that scientists have found a "cure" for AIDS.

Anyone who works in any area of reproductive health must remember the urgent and global need for effective HIV prevention strategies, and that this need will be with us for many years to come. For those who work primarily with family planning, seeking creative ways to incorporate appropriate, cost-effective sexually transmitted disease (STD)/HIV prevention activities into their programs must continue to be a priority. Promoting condom use among clients at risk of a sexually transmitted disease is just one example of how family planning providers in many countries are already making an important contribution to HIV prevention.

No Replacement

Although powerful antiviral drug combinations will make it possible to improve and extend life for many who are infected with HIV, drug treatment will never replace prevention. These therapies are already proving unaffordable for poor and underinsured North Americans. The cost—at least U.S. $10,000 per patient per year—guarantees that they will not be accessible to most people with HIV/AIDS in developing countries, where 90 percent of all HIV infections occur. Even for those who can afford them, the drug "cocktails" are not a cure. We do not know how long they can keep the virus in check, and the drugs do not work for everybody. Moreover, compliance is difficult: the three drugs must be taken several times a day with more than a liter of water, some on an empty stomach and others with a high-fat meal.

The cost and complexity of the three-drug regimen and the remarkable ability of HIV to mutate more rapidly than any other known virus raises the specter of multiple drug resistance. If patients do not take the drugs correctly, or if treatment is interrupted because of adverse side effects or a patient's inability to afford a new prescription, strains of HIV will develop that are resistant to many, if not most, of the limited number of drugs currently available. These resistant strains will be transmitted to others, making the drug combinations powerless against HIV even in people who have never taken them.

Further research will undoubtedly lead to more effective HIV/AIDS treatments that are easier for patients to take, and we must fight to make these treatments accessible to all. One possibility is a two-tiered pricing system to make the new drug combinations affordable in developing countries. Companies that reap huge profits from HIV/AIDS drugs in industrialized countries have a moral obligation to work with governments, nongovernmental organizations (NGOs) and people living with HIV/AIDS to expand access to these life-saving therapies.

Support for HIV prevention research could pay even greater dividends. Through applied research by HIV/AIDS prevention projects around the world, we know that the three main strategies of Family Health International's AIDS Control and Prevention (AIDSCAP) project and the Joint United Nations Programme on HIV/AIDS (UNAIDS)— communication to change behavior, condom promotion and improved STD services—can reduce transmission of the virus. Studies sponsored by the U.S. National Institutes of Health-funded HIVNET (HIV Network for Efficacy Trials) Consortium in nine international sites managed by Family Health International will identify new tools to complement these three strategies in developing countries. Methods under study include vaccines, microbicides, new approaches to counseling, and prophylactic perinatal drugs.

Prevention Works

Clearly, universal access to effective, affordable antiviral therapy is a distant goal. But the good news—news that has made few headlines—is that we can reduce the need for treatment. Data show that HIV prevention works—and at a fraction of the cost of drug treatment.

As in basic and clinical research on HIV/AIDS, years of painstaking research and practice in prevention are beginning to pay off. For more than a decade, public health professionals and educators have been refining effective approaches to slowing the spread of HIV.

We have figured out which strategies work and how to make them culturally sensitive, politically acceptable and economically feasible in some of the least developed regions of the world.

We have learned that some populations—among them, women and young people—are particularly vulnerable and require special programs that address their needs. And we've found out how to work with grass-roots organizations with strong community ties to ensure that prevention efforts can be sustained.

Lower Infection Rates

Here is what we have discovered:

Prevention education and communication can reduce risky behavior. Education, counseling and communication campaigns give people the knowledge, skills and support they need to prevent HIV transmission. In Uganda, for example, the "ABC" message (abstinence, behavior change or condoms) is reaching young people through schools, community outreach and the media, and a 35 percent decrease in HIV prevalence among young women attending antenatal clinics suggests a substantial reduction in new HIV infections among 15- to 24-year-old girls and women from 1990–93 to 1994–95.

In the United States, Australia and Western Europe, HIV

incidence appears to be stabilizing, largely because of effective prevention efforts within gay communities. Even while in the Rwandan refugee camps, where the daily struggle for survival made AIDS seem a distant threat, many have responded to prevention education by becoming more faithful to their partners.

Treating sexually transmitted diseases helps prevent HIV transmission. The presence of preventable STDs increases susceptibility to HIV infection as much as ninefold. Groundbreaking research in Tanzania has confirmed that STD treatment can reduce HIV transmission by more than 40 percent. This could make a big difference in the developing world, where most of the curable sexually transmitted infections occur.

Asay. © by *Colorado Springs Sun*. Reprinted by permission of Copley News Service.

Promoting condom use results in lower infection rates. In Thailand, aggressive condom promotion throughout the country and tough enforcement of condom use in brothels led to reductions in transmission of HIV and other STDs. Skyrocketing condom sales in countries where condoms could hardly be given away just 10 years ago are another indicator of the success of HIV prevention interventions.

Social marketing programs that make condoms more accessible and attractive to potential users have increased condom sales in countries from Haiti to Ethiopia to Nepal. In sub-Saharan Africa, annual condom sales rose from less than 1 million in 1988 to more than 167 million in 1995.

Policy Changes

Encouraging national policy change makes HIV prevention possible. Adopting policies that support rather than obstruct prevention efforts is one of the most important ways a government can protect its citizens from HIV infection. In Brazil, condom sales boomed after the government eliminated a 15 percent tariff on imported condoms. The Thai government's "100 Percent Condom Policy," which encourages consistent condom use among sex workers, has contributed to decreases in HIV and STD transmission, and has inspired similar efforts in the Philippines and the Dominican Republic. Throughout the world, when government leaders have spoken out about HIV/AIDS prevention, their openness has encouraged a more vigorous response to the epidemic.

Strengthening indigenous AIDS prevention organizations is the best way to reach communities and sustain prevention efforts. From 1991 to 1995, when political unrest and an international trade embargo paralyzed Haiti, Haitian nongovernmental organizations valiantly continued the prevention effort. With support from FHI's AIDSCAP Project, funded by the U.S. Agency for International Development, these small groups initiated effective prevention programs in workplaces, schools, churches and community centers, reaching both urban and rural populations. And in Tanzania, AIDSCAP has helped NGOs abandon competition and collaborate on prevention programs in the regions of the country most affected by HIV/AIDS.

Comprehensive HIV prevention programs have the greatest impact. Experience has shown that combining these prevention approaches multiplies their effectiveness, creating a social and political environment that supports sustained behavior change and reduced risk. Just as combination HIV therapies are more effective against the virus in infected individuals, combination HIV prevention approaches have a greater impact on the virus in populations where it is prevalent. Family planning professionals have a vital role to play in this comprehensive approach.

Best Investment

Despite the success of these prevention strategies, and the continued elusiveness of an effective and affordable cure or vaccine, only a small percentage of the funding for global HIV/AIDS efforts goes to prevention programs. Yet even when an effective vaccine against HIV becomes available, it will not be perfect, and we will still need all the other prevention approaches working together in combination. Thus, these combination HIV prevention strategies in populations are analogous to our need for combination HIV treatment approaches in individuals.

This need is now greater than ever. As many as 40 million people will have been infected with HIV by the end of the 1990s. In some regions, entire generations will be devastated by the disease, leaving behind hundreds of thousands of orphans dependent on charity and social services. As workers in their most productive years succumb to AIDS and national health budgets are stretched thin by the rising cost of caring for the ill, the economic fallout will strain the struggling economies of developing nations. These pressures on fragile societies can intensify political unrest and instability.

If we fail to support HIV prevention while waiting for a medical "magic bullet," the consequences will be catastrophic. As we applaud biomedical advances in AIDS research, we must not forget that HIV prevention remains one of the best investments we can make in a healthier, more productive and more stable world.

Periodical Bibliography

The following articles have been selected to supplement the diverse views presented in this chapter.

Sara Altshul	"Protect Yourself Against HIV," *Prevention*, September 2001.
Richard T. Andria and Robert E. Stein	"Sterile Syringes and Needle Exchange Programs," *Human Rights*, July 1997.
David Baltimore	"Can We Make an AIDS Vaccine?" *National Forum*, June 1999.
Tim Beardsley	"Lives in the Balance," *Scientific American*, April 1998.
Jon Cohen	"AIDS Vaccines Show Promise After Years of Frustration," *Science*, March 2, 2001.
Jon Cohen	"Disappointing Data Scuttle Plans for Large-Scale AIDS Vaccine Trial," *Science*, March 1, 2002.
Geoffrey Cowley	"Can He Find a Cure?" *Newsweek*, June 11, 2001.
Jon Fuller	"Needle Exchange: Saving Lives," *America*, July 18, 1998.
Christine Gorman	"If the Condom Breaks," *Time*, June 23, 1997.
Marjorie Heins	"Sex, Lies and Politics," *Nation*, May 7, 2001.
Patricia Kahn	"Dying for a Vaccine," *Poz*, July 1998.
Michael D. Lemonick and Alice Park	"Vaccines Stage a Comeback," *Time*, January 21, 2002.
Joe Loconte	"Killing Them Softly," *Policy Review*, July/August 1998.
Jim Mitulski	"Catholic Ethicists on HIV/AIDS Prevention," *Christian Century*, July 18, 2001.
Sheryl Gay Stolberg	"Abstinence-Only Initiative Advancing," *New York Times*, February 28, 2002.
Meredith Wadman	"How Close Is the AIDS Vaccine?" *Fortune*, November 13, 2000.
Bruce G. Weniger and Max Essex	"Clearing the Way for an AIDS Vaccine," *New York Times*, January 4, 1997.

CHAPTER 4

How Should AIDS Be Treated?

Chapter Preface

HIV mutates so quickly that it soon becomes resistant to a single drug used against it. Researchers discovered that using two drugs was fairly effective in preventing HIV from overcoming the body's immune system, but even better was a combination of three drugs. Such drug "cocktails" emerged in 1996 as a successful treatment to combat HIV/AIDS. David Ho, a prominent AIDS researcher, also began advocating a new treatment approach to HIV: "Hit it hard and hit it early." Ho hoped that if drug cocktails (hitting it hard) were used against the virus as soon as it was detected (hitting it early), the patient would be completely free of HIV in a few years. According to Ho, science and past experience supported his new treatment plan. He asks, "Do you wait for any other kind of infection to get really bad before you treat it? Of course not."

People with AIDS (PWAs) are living longer now due to the new treatment regimens such as drug cocktails. While this is good news, tests show that HIV is never totally eradicated from the body. The drug cocktails hold the virus in check or else reduce the viral loads to levels that cannot be detected by current testing methods, but HIV is never completely gone. If the drug regimen is stopped, HIV rebounds rapidly. Since HIV can not be eradicated, PWAs must continue to take the drugs for the rest of their lives. Unfortunately, the drugs used in the anti-HIV cocktails are extremely toxic, and patients face adverse side effects, such as nausea, diarrhea, heart disease, and other uncomfortable, disfiguring, or dangerous problems. Some researchers also believe that beginning treatment early may increase the chance that HIV will become resistant to the drugs.

Although some analysts believe that the side effects of AIDS drugs can actually cause death, others contend that AIDS drugs have helped many PWAs live longer. In the following chapter, the authors offer different views on the safety and efficacy of AIDS drugs, who should take them, and whether scientists will develop a cure for AIDS that will make such drugs unnecessary.

"There is simply no scientific evidence demonstrating that [AIDS is a disease caused by a virus called HIV]."

The Assumption That HIV Causes AIDS Hinders Treatment

Kary B. Mullis

Kary B. Mullis performed research on human immunodeficiency virus (HIV) and won the Nobel Prize for chemistry in 1993. In the following viewpoint, he argues that it has not been proven that HIV causes AIDS. He has searched unsuccessfully for years for any scientific study that definitively shows that the virus is the cause of AIDS. He also asserts that AIDS experts have been unable to provide any evidence that HIV causes AIDS.

As you read, consider the following questions:
1. Why did the author feel he needed a reference for the statement "HIV is the probable cause of AIDS"?
2. Who is Peter Duesberg, according to the author?
3. What is AZT, as explained by Mullis?

Kary B. Mullis, foreword, *Inventing the AIDS Virus*, by Peter H. Duesberg (New York: Regnery Publishing, 1996).Copyright © 1996 by Kary B. Mullis. Reproduced with permission.

In 1988 I was working as a consultant at Specialty Labs in Santa Monica, setting up analytic routines for the Human Immunodeficiency Virus (HIV). I knew a lot about setting up analytic routines for anything with nucleic acids in it because I had invented the Polymerase Chain Reaction. That's why they had hired me.

Acquired Immune Deficiency Syndrome (AIDS), on the other hand, was something I did not know a lot about. Thus, when I found myself writing a report on our progress and goals for the project, sponsored by the National Institutes of Health, I recognized that I did not know the scientific reference to support a statement I had just written: "HIV is the probable cause of AIDS."

Looking for the Reference

So I turned to the virologist at the next desk, a reliable and competent fellow, and asked him for the reference. He said I didn't need one. I disagreed. While it's true that certain scientific discoveries or techniques are so well established that their sources are no longer referenced in the contemporary literature, that didn't seem to be the case with the HIV/AIDS connection. It was totally remarkable to me that the individual who had discovered the cause of a deadly and as-yet-uncured disease would not be continually referenced in the scientific papers until that disease was cured and forgotten. But as I would soon learn, the name of that individual—who would surely be Nobel material—was on the tip of no one's tongue.

Of course, this simple reference had to be out there *somewhere*. Otherwise, tens of thousands of public servants and esteemed scientists of many callings, trying to solve the tragic deaths of a large number of homosexual and/or intravenous (IV) drug-using men between the ages of twenty-five and forty, would not have allowed their research to settle into one narrow channel of investigation. Everyone wouldn't fish in the same pond unless it was well established that all the other ponds were empty. There had to be a published paper, or perhaps several of them, which taken together indicated that HIV was the probable cause of AIDS. There just had to be.

I did computer searches, but came up with nothing. Of course, you can miss something important in computer searches by not putting in just the right key words. To be certain about a scientific issue, it's best to ask other scientists directly. That's one thing that scientific conferences in faraway places with nice beaches are *for*.

I was going to a lot of meetings and conferences as part of my job. I got in the habit of approaching anyone who gave a talk about AIDS and asking him or her what reference I should quote for that increasingly problematic statement, "HIV is the probable cause of AIDS."

After ten or fifteen meetings over a couple years, I was getting pretty upset when *no one* could cite the reference. I didn't like the ugly conclusion that was forming in my mind: The entire campaign against a disease increasingly regarded as a twentieth-century Black Plague was based on a hypothesis whose origins no one could recall. That defied both scientific and common sense.

Still No Answer

Finally, I had an opportunity to question one of the giants in HIV and AIDS research, Dr. Luc Montagnier of the Pasteur Institute, when he gave a talk in San Diego. It would be the last time I would be able to ask my little question without showing anger, and I figured Montagnier would know the answer. So I asked him.

With a look of condescending puzzlement, Montagnier said, "Why don't you quote the report from the Centers for Disease Control?"

I replied, "It doesn't really address the issue of whether or not HIV is the probable cause of AIDS, does it?"

"No," he admitted, no doubt wondering when I would just go away. He looked for support to the little circle of people around him, but they were all awaiting a more definitive response, like I was.

"Why don't you quote the work on SIV [Simian Immunodeficiency Virus]?" the good doctor offered.

"I read that too, Dr. Montagnier," I responded. "What happened to those monkeys didn't remind me of AIDS. Besides, that paper was just published only a couple of months ago. I'm looking for the *original* paper where somebody showed that HIV caused AIDS."

This time, Dr. Montagnier's response was to walk quickly away to greet an acquaintance across the room.

The Evidence Against HIV

Were the HIV virus the author of AIDS, it would be found invading the white blood cells of the immune system of the AIDS patient, in particular the T cells, at a rate exceeding that at which the patient's body could replace them. Virus particles, or virions, would in such case be found in great quantities in the patient's bloodstream. But virions can be found nowhere at all in the bodies of most AIDS patients, and in the contrary cases the numbers found are of vanishing order.

Indeed, HIV testing is a search not for active HIV viruses but for HIV antibodies. Which is to say, an HIV-positive outcome of this instructive and amusing test signifies that whatever disease is actually caused by the HIV virus, it is one that has already run its course. As for the notion that the virus goes into hiding somewhere in the body, lurking there for years, no such hiding place has ever been found, despite that it has been assiduously sought.

Patrick M. Meehan, *Washington Times*, June 27, 1999.

Cut to the scene inside my car just a few years ago. I was driving from Mendocino to San Diego. Like everyone else by now, I knew a lot more about AIDS than I wanted to. But I still didn't know who had determined that it was caused by HIV. Getting sleepy as I came over the San Bernardino Mountains, I switched on the radio and tuned in a guy who was talking about AIDS. His name was Peter Duesberg, and he was a prominent virologist at Berkeley. I'd heard of him, but had never read his papers or heard him speak. But I listened, now wide awake, while he explained exactly why I was having so much trouble finding the references that linked HIV to AIDS. *There weren't any.* No one had ever proved that HIV causes AIDS. When I got home, I invited Duesberg down to San Diego to present his ideas to a meeting of the American Association for Chemistry. Mostly skeptical at first, the audience stayed for the lecture, and then an hour of questions, and then stayed talking to each other until requested to clear the room. Everyone left with more questions than they had brought.

I like and respect Peter Duesberg. I don't think he knows necessarily what causes AIDS; we have disagreements about that. But we're both certain about what *doesn't* cause AIDS.

No Scientific Evidence

We have not been able to discover any good reasons why most of the people on earth believe that AIDS is a disease caused by a virus called *HIV.* There is simply no scientific evidence demonstrating that this is true.

We have also not been able to discover why doctors prescribe a *toxic* drug called *AZT* (Zidovudine) to people who have no other complaint than the presence of antibodies to HIV in their blood. In fact, we cannot understand why humans would take that drug for any reason.

We cannot understand how all this madness came about, and having both lived in Berkeley, we've seen some strange things indeed. We know that to err is human, but the HIV/AIDS hypothesis is one hell of a mistake.

I say this rather strongly as a warning. Duesberg has been saying it for a long time.

| "*No patients develop or die from AIDS in whom the virus cannot be detected by currently available techniques.*"

HIV Is the Cause of AIDS

Lyn R. Frumkin and John M. Leonard

AIDS is a disease that encompasses many different illnesses, but every person with AIDS has one common factor, according to authors Lyn R. Frumkin and John M. Leonard. They assert in the following viewpoint that each person with AIDS has the human immunodeficiency virus (HIV). They argue that HIV must be the cause of AIDS because every person who dies of AIDS has the virus. In addition, the amount of HIV in a person's blood determines how quickly the disease progresses; high amounts of the virus will sicken and kill the patient faster than low amounts of the virus. Further proof that HIV causes AIDS is the fact that AIDS transmission through blood transfusion has been essentially eliminated since blood meant for transfusion has been screened for HIV. Frumkin and Leonard are the authors of *Questions and Answers on AIDS*.

As you read, consider the following questions:
1. What does the acronym AIDS mean, and why was the disease given that name, according to Frumkin and Leonard?
2. When was the first reported case of AIDS, as cited by the authors?
3. What is the most compelling evidence for the authors that HIV causes AIDS?

In 1981 unusual infections were identified in a small number of homosexual men in California and New York. The infections responded poorly to therapy and ended in the death of the patient. Because none of the patients suffered from any condition known to predispose to infections, physicians concluded that the patients had developed an illness never before described in the medical literature. The new condition was named the Acquired Immunodeficiency Syndrome, or AIDS.

What Is AIDS?

The name *AIDS* acknowledged all of the fundamental characteristics of the illness, in particular the underlying impairment of the immune system and resulting inability to fight infections. The word *acquired* was chosen because the illness was not inherited or the result of other recognized conditions; the illness developed during a period of health with no identifiable explanation for the immunodeficiency. The word *syndrome* signified that the disease could present with many different clinical manifestations but that the affected patients ultimately had the same underlying illness. A syndrome is a constellation of findings that when combined, indicate the presence of a particular illness. For example, persons with AIDS have illnesses that range from cancer in one patient to pneumonia in the next, although in both cases the illnesses occur as the result of the same problem. It became apparent that immune deficiency was the common denominator linking the different illnesses in patients with AIDS.

Several years elapsed between the first reports of AIDS and the identification of the virus that caused it, the human immunodeficiency virus (HIV). The isolation of HIV provided an explanation for the transmission patterns of AIDS as well as the immune deficiency. The name *acquired immunodeficiency syndrome* was selected in 1981 to describe what scientists and the medical community knew about the illness at the time that it was named. The term *AIDS* is now a part of everyday speech.

AIDS was unrecognized in organized medicine before it was first reported in 1981. Since the identification of HIV as the cause of AIDS, tests on stored blood found HIV infection in samples from central Africa collected as early as 1959. In other regions, poorly understood cases that occurred years before the AIDS epidemic have now been identified as AIDS, indicating that isolated cases of AIDS occurred in Europe and the United States since the 1960s. The existence of AIDS before the late 1950s is speculative, although it may have existed elsewhere in the world for many years far from the observation of Western physicians. From the perspective of modern medicine, however, AIDS is a newly recognized illness.

Transmissible animal illnesses characterized by severely altered immunity were well known before AIDS appeared in humans. Some of these animal illnesses had been studied for years and provided the impetus to search for a viral cause of AIDS. The spread of AIDS outside the male homosexual population further supported the theory that a transmissible agent caused AIDS. The search for the causative agent culminated in the discovery of a virus in 1983 at the Pasteur Institute in France. The discoverers of this new virus named it *Lymphadenopathy Associated Virus (LAV)*. Shortly after the French discovery, two American laboratories corroborated the initial finding and called their viruses *Human T-cell Lymphotropic Virus III (HTLV-III)* and *AIDS-Associated Retrovirus (ARV)*. An international committee agreed to rename the virus *human immunodeficiency virus (HIV)* in 1987.

What Is the Evidence That HIV Causes AIDS?

A substantial body of evidence widely accepted by scientists and physicians alike supports HIV as the causative agent of AIDS. HIV is routinely isolated from individuals who have AIDS and AIDS-related illnesses. Improved virus detection techniques uniformly find HIV in virtually all patients with AIDS. The mere isolation of HIV, however, is not proof that it causes illness. Some have argued that HIV is only a passenger found in the blood and that it does not cause AIDS. Proponents of this theory claim that although HIV is found in patients with AIDS, there are other risk factors, usually either recreational drug use or some other as yet undiscovered factor associated with sexual promiscuity, that are the true cause of AIDS. This argument has lost scientific credibility because of the overwhelming evidence in support of HIV infection as the cause of AIDS. There is no agent other than HIV that even remotely accounts for the patterns of transmission of the disease, the means of disease production (called the pathogenesis of AIDS), and the clinical response to therapy observed when the growth of HIV is inhibited by drugs.

AIDS and HIV Infection Are Linked

Many studies agree that only a single factor, HIV, predicts whether a person will develop AIDS.

Other viral infections, bacterial infections, sexual behavior patterns and drug abuse patterns do not predict who develops AIDS. Individuals from diverse backgrounds, including heterosexual men and women, homosexual men and women, hemophiliacs, sexual partners of hemophiliacs and transfusion recipients, injection-drug users and infants have all developed AIDS, with the only common denominator being their infection with HIV.

In cohort studies, severe immunosuppression and AIDS-defining illnesses occur almost exclusively in individuals who are HIV-infected.

For example, analysis of data from more than 8,000 participants in the Multicenter AIDS Cohort Study (MACS) and the Women's Interagency HIV Study (WIHS) demonstrated that participants who were HIV-seropositive were 1,100 times more likely to develop an AIDS-associated illness than those who were HIV-seronegative. These overwhelming odds provide a clarity of association that is unusual in medical research.

National Institute of Allergy and Infectious Diseases, National Institute of Health, *The Evidence That HIV Causes AIDS*, updated November 29, 2000.

Perhaps the most compelling evidence for HIV as the cause of AIDS comes from studies in which people are followed over time. First, no patients develop or die from AIDS in whom the virus cannot be detected by currently available techniques. Second, the rate at which individuals progress to and die from AIDS is directly related to the amount of HIV present in the blood stream. Patients without HIV never develop AIDS; patients with low levels of virus progress slowly to AIDS; and, patients with high levels of virus progress quickly to AIDS. Other related evidence implicating HIV as the causative agent of AIDS comes from clinical trials that test drugs active against HIV. Regimens composed of drugs with potent activity against HIV prove that reducing the quantity of HIV present in blood uniformly reduces the rate at which patients progress to AIDS. These trials show that less virus leads to less HIV-related disease over time.

In addition to the nearly universal detection of HIV in patients with AIDS, meticulous studies indicate that HIV is not found outside of groups who are at risk for AIDS. Therefore, there is a very tight association between infection with HIV and both people who have AIDS and those at risk for AIDS. Many individuals found to be infected with HIV have no evidence of disease at the time of virus isolation. Detailed longitudinal studies of such people indicate that with sufficient time, most will ultimately develop AIDS. The unusual cases of long-term non-progressors (individuals with long-standing HIV infection but little clinical evidence of HIV-related disease), do not undermine HIV as the causative agent of AIDS. Studies of these individuals suggest that HIV isolated from their blood, their immune response to HIV, or both, are qualitatively different when compared with patients who have a more typical progression to AIDS. Attenuated HIV growth characteristics and an aggressive immune response to virus in patients with slow progression to disease support HIV as the causative agent of AIDS. Furthermore, laboratory work provides another form of evidence that HIV causes AIDS. Scientists showed that HIV infects and kills CD4 T-cells, the same type of lymphocyte that is depleted in people with AIDS.

Deliberately inoculating an uninfected person with HIV and observing the development of AIDS would constitute definite proof that HIV is the cause of AIDS. Although this type of inoculation will never be performed, situations that approximate direct inoculation have occurred inadvertently. Before the introduction of blood-screening procedures, direct inoculation occurred in people who unknowingly received HIV via a blood transfusion; these individuals subsequently developed AIDS and AIDS-related illnesses. Efforts to eliminate HIV from the blood supply have nearly eliminated blood transfusion as a means of transmitting HIV and with that, have essentially eliminated blood transfusion as a source of AIDS. This is further proof that HIV causes AIDS.

"*That most publicly posed of questions— Can HIV be eradicated?—now has an answer: No.*"

AIDS Cannot Be Cured

Mike Barr

In the mid-1990s, it was believed that a cure would soon be found for AIDS. Researchers discovered, however, that drugs that at one time looked promising as a cure were unable to completely eradicate HIV from the victim's bloodstream. In the following viewpoint, Mike Barr, a writer for *Poz*, a magazine for people with AIDS (PWAs), examines the history of the search for a cure. He reports that studies have found that as long as a PWA takes drugs, the HIV is controlled, but as soon as the drug regimen is stopped, the virus quickly returns. Many scientists now believe that HIV infection is forever. However, Barr asserts, there is cause for optimism: Drugs and treatment programs currently available can keep HIV under control.

As you read, consider the following questions:

1. According to Barr, what were the earliest estimates for how long HIV had to be treated until it was eradicated from the body?
2. What is a realistic scenario for the treatment of HIV infection, according to Barr?
3. What is "subtraction theory," as cited by the author?

Mike Barr, "God Is Dead," *Poz*, March 1998. Copyright © 1998 by Mike Barr. Reproduced with permission.

S o it's official. The "cure" isn't the cure. That most publicly posed of questions—Can HIV be eradicated?—now
has an answer: No. After the disappointing findings of three
major studies published in November 1997, the verdict is in:
Whether driven by cynical manipulation or misguided good
intentions, eradication is a fantasy.

How we wanted and needed to believe! Yet no sooner had
Dr. David Ho, the toast of Vancouver and *Time*'s 1996 Man
of the Year, tantalized the planet than his ever-elusive cure
began to fade. With each passing season's scientific conference, it slipped further from our grasp. Early in 1997, Eradication Inc. declared two to three years' treatment enough to
wipe out HIV infection; by spring 1997, it was six years; in
fall 1997, a decade or more.

The Virus Lives On

And then the model imploded. Buried in the footnotes to the
headlines of therapeutic euphoria were two fundamental
preconditions: That the current cocktails shut down viral
replication 100 percent in all parts of the body, and that the
cells already pirated by the virus grow old and die before the
patient does. Neither is true.

Taken together, the three studies—each by a leading researcher—report ongoing, low-level viral replication, the
persistent presence of infectious cells and at least one type of
infected CD4 whose numbers never so much as dwindle.
Even in someone whose viral load has been undetectable
(less than 200) for 30 months, the virus lives on; stop therapy, and—at least in the lab—it can return, raging.

If the cure doesn't exist, what is to be done? Is it time,
once again, to charge our credit cards to the limit? Or can
life go on without eradication? Experts disagree. Hard-
nosed realists argue that viral eradication was never even a
possibility. "Can HIV be eradicated?" was the wrong question, they say. These determined empiricists have maintained all along that HIV infection is forever. A more realistic scenario would be to maintain HIV at levels low enough
to spare the immune system and allow the virus and its host
to peaceably coexist—with or without treatment. Follow
this line of thought, and the apotheosis of eradication sacri-

Eradication Is Premature

It is premature to as yet accept the notion that we can "eradicate" HIV or are about to turn HIV into a chronic manageable disease. These early suggestions of that are based on an incomplete and small body of research. Some of the studies upon which this notion is based are small uncontrolled pilot studies, about whose study designs I have some questions. The results are promising, but further studies need to be properly designed and implemented before we place too much stock in them. Confirmation of these theories can only come from a variety of comprehensive additional trials that need to explore a number of related issues.

National AIDS Treatment Advocacy Project, "Can HIV Be 'Eradicated' from the Infected Individual?" June 28, 1996.

fices the lion's share of its mystique.

Eradication or not, nothing in the bleak ramifications of these three experiments in any way undoes the renewed well-being and Lazarus-like returns of thousands of PWAs (People with AIDS) over the past two years. Many who had a mere 10 to 20 CD4 cells in 1995 now have 200 or more. And with viral loads dramatically reduced, once-ravaged immune systems can now function at a satisfactory level. But with the twilight of the eradication ideology, it is doubtful that the current rush to treat is in the long-term interest of asymptomatics with a moderate viral load and an intact immune system. For anyone who has not yet bought a ticket to the triple-cocktail lottery, waiting even six to 12 months to embark upon this uncharted pharmaceutical odyssey may make a world of difference: In 1998 we may finally figure out what harm and good these drugs are actually doing and have regimens that are easier to start and stick to.

New Treatment Theories

For the hordes who have already succumbed to the pressure to "hit it early and hard," it's more important than ever to take this pill-popping business seriously. But the bravest of the lucky ones—those with "undetectable" viral loads for 12 to 18 months or more—might consider a leap off the edge of the known treatment map into "subtraction" therapy: Reducing or switching a three- or four-drug combo to a two-

or one-drug regimen. The idea—highly speculative—is that once the virus has been brought to its knees, a less aggressive assault may keep it down. Toss out the protease inhibitor (or the 3TC) before resistance develops, and you may be able to use them in the future.

While right now the drug pipeline is as empty as Mother Hubbard's cupboard for all but antiretroviral virgins, there are enough new approaches for a scintilla of optimism. The pleasant surprises of the eradication era have infused us all with a new energy that we mustn't lose. If the antiretroviral approaches have taken us as far as they can, so be it: Now immunological and cellular approaches must carry us the rest of the way. With vigilance and advocacy, these therapies could be available in a year or two. All we have to do is stay well until then.

"The only alternative to pursuing a cure is to give up on a cure. And that's not an option."

The Search for an AIDS Cure Must Continue

Mark Schoofs

Early optimism about curing AIDS has proven to be premature, and long-term treatment with powerful drugs is unrealistic, asserts Mark Schoofs in the following viewpoint. Yet new strategies are constantly being devised and tested for fighting HIV/AIDS. He reports that one new treatment program plans to use drugs to suppress the virus while a vaccine is administered to boost the patient's immune system. Even if this treatment is unsuccessful, Schoofs maintains that scientists must continue to test new therapies. The only other alternative is to give up searching for a cure, an option he contends is unacceptable. Schoofs is a writer for the *Village Voice*.

As you read, consider the following questions:

1. How long does David Ho think it may take the body to clear HIV out of immune system cells, as cited by Schoofs?
2. In the author's opinion, why is it not enough to suppress HIV with drugs currently available?
3. What does Schoofs say is the difference between a patient with HIV who dies four years after being infected and one that shows no sign of the disease after eighteen years?

Almost three years ago (in 1995), top AIDS researcher David Ho was beginning the trial that would make eradication of HIV the goal of AIDS therapy. The idea was simple: Powerful drug combinations, including the new protease inhibitors, were able to stop the virus from replicating. Ho hoped the body would do the rest of the work, by clearing out all the cells infected with HIV.

"It's like a chess game," Ho said at the time. "If we are lucky enough to win, then great. But if we don't, understanding the moves the virus would make is still pretty useful."

HIV's Next Move

Well, now we've seen HIV's next move. The vast majority of virus is indeed cleared by the body, but a tiny amount hides in certain immune system cells, where it lurks, dormant but able to reignite infection. Before this discovery, Ho estimated that HIV might be cleared in two years. Now, because HIV's accomplice cells persist in the body for a long time, he thinks it could take up to 20 years.

Unfortunately, it's not realistic to expect most patients to stay for that long on the powerful drugs—which are now being found to have significant side effects, and which must be taken on a strict schedule to prevent resistance. Bottom line: Suppressing the virus with current drugs isn't enough.

How, then, can doctors cure AIDS? They could try to flush out the Trojan-horse cells that harbor the virus. Several teams are trying this strategy, but the drugs they're using inflame the immune system, causing flulike symptoms. Patients would likely have to endure several bouts of this treatment, yet at the end of it all, HIV might still be hiding in sanctuary cells the drugs don't reach.

But if doctors could strengthen the immune system so it can control small amounts of HIV, then every last virus wouldn't have to be eliminated. And that might make a cure a lot more feasible.

T-Cells

Bruce Walker, a researcher at Massachusetts General Hospital, tells a tale of two patients. One died just four years after he first got infected, the other shows no signs of disease after 18 years. What's the difference?

T-cells. These are the command-and-control arm of the immune system, marshaling attacks against invading germs. But each of the body's billions of T-cells recognizes only one germ—the flu virus, for example, or the tuberculosis bacterium. People with HIV whose immune systems never deteriorate retain T-cells that recognize the virus. But the vast majority of AIDS patients quickly lose their HIV-specific T-cells. As a result, the body cannot keep the virus under control, and the patient sickens and dies.

A Vaccine Will Be Found

While daunting challenges remain, AIDS vaccine research has amassed a remarkable amount of new knowledge in a relatively short period of time, and evidence from immunological, epidemiological, and animal studies continue to suggest that an AIDS vaccine is a realistic possibility. Inevitably, there will be scientists who will discover the crucial components of a successful AIDS vaccine. How long it takes to make those essential discoveries—and to control the assault of HIV/AIDS on humankind—will depend on the number and quality of scientists committed to the goal of finding an AIDS vaccine and on the level of resources provided in support of their work.

American Foundation for AIDS Research, *Annual Report*, 1999.

Recently, Walker found that if he treated people very soon after they were infected, suppressing their virus completely, these patients were able to preserve their HIV-specific T-cell response. Indeed, their immune systems appear identical to those of long-term non-progressors.

But are they really the same? The acid test will be to take these quickly treated patients off therapy and see if they can control the virus. But even if they could keep HIV in check, the advance would not be very practical. Most people don't rush into care right after being infected—and that's especially true as the disease increasingly afflicts poor people who don't have access to good medical care. So the real question is whether people infected for a long time, whose HIV-specific T-cells have been wiped out, can get them back.

Vaccines

One approach is to take immune system cells out of the body, alter them in test tubes so that they recognize HIV, and then put them back. But Walker and Ho are trying to alter immune cells without removing them from the body. Their instrument? Vaccines, which train the immune system to recognize invaders.

Using an AIDS vaccine for therapy has been tried before, most notably by Jonas Salk. But until recently, drugs couldn't suppress the AIDS virus, so the vaccines had to work in the midst of a raging HIV infection. Not surprisingly, they failed.

But now, with powerful drugs controlling the virus, Walker, Ho, and other researchers are about to start human trials using HIV vaccines to boost the immune system. Scientists are encouraged by signs that, on therapy, the immune system makes a slow comeback, even if it has been ravaged by the disease for years. But except in patients treated very early, it almost never returns to full strength. So can the immune system really be trained to cope with a virus as vicious as HIV?

Time and again in AIDS, promising ideas have been shattered by reality. The result is that the C-word—*cure*—has become a lightning rod. Utter it and you're bound to stir up a storm, as Ho has by championing the possibility of eradication.

What's really at stake here is raising false hopes—and, indeed, the vaccine approach may fail. But so what? The only alternative to pursuing a cure is to give up on a cure. And that's not an option.

*"Being diagnosed with AIDS is no longer
the equivalent of a death sentence."*

AIDS Drugs Can Prolong Lives

Ruth Larson

The survival time of a person diagnosed with AIDS has increased greatly in the past few years, according to Ruth Larson in the following viewpoint. In fact, she adds, AIDS is no longer among the top ten causes of death. However, medical advances in treating AIDS have led to other problems, Larson notes. Social and support services are increasingly strained as people with AIDS live longer, forcing the services to stretch budgets, resources, and staff. Larson is a reporter for the *Washington Times*.

As you read, consider the following questions:

1. AIDS deaths dropped by what percent between 1996 and 1997, according to the author?
2. What reason does Anthony Fauci give for the decline in deaths and complications among AIDS patients?
3. What are some of the drawbacks to taking AIDS cocktails, as cited by Larson?

Ruth Larson, "Good News, Bad News for Patients with AIDS," *Washington Times*, February 9, 1999. Copyright © 1999 by *Washington Times*. Reproduced with permission.

B eing diagnosed with AIDS is no longer the equivalent of a death sentence, but people with AIDS are finding that living longer brings a host of new challenges.

In 1989, someone diagnosed with AIDS could expect to live three years at most, said Craig Shniderman, executive director of Food & Friends, an organization that prepares specialized meals for people with AIDS in the metropolitan Washington D.C. area.

But in the last five years, medical advances have given people with AIDS both the opportunities and the problems that come with living longer lives, he said.

"I can't tell you how many stories I've heard of the 25-year-old who learns he has AIDS, so he goes out and buys a car and goes on vacation, because he thinks he's going to die," Mr. Shniderman recalled. "Then all of a sudden, he's not going to die, and he's got a load of credit-card debt."

AIDS Deaths Are Declining

Between 1996 and 1997, the number of deaths caused by HIV-AIDS infections dropped by 47 percent, marking the lowest rate since figures first became available in 1987. HIV-AIDS infection had been one of the top 10 causes of death in this country since 1989; by 1997, it had dropped to 14th place.

From 1995 to 1998, deaths and complications from AIDS dropped by 81 percent among homosexual males, and by 60 percent among heterosexuals, according to a study by researchers at Johns Hopkins University.

The reason, said AIDS researcher Dr. Anthony Fauci, is the availability of potent drugs that can block the replication of the virus. "There is less suppression of the immune response, or the immune system is able to rebound to fight the virus."

"That's the good news. The sobering news is, that's not the end of the problem," said Dr. Fauci, head of the National Institute of Allergy and Infectious Diseases. Many AIDS patients respond well to initial treatments, but then a drug-resistant form of the virus returns.

"These drugs are powerful, but they don't completely suppress the virus," Dr. Fauci said.

There are also drawbacks to the so-called AIDS cocktails—combinations of drugs to combat the disease. Keeping AIDS at bay means taking an imposing array of drugs on a strict schedule, as well as following special diets.

"People have been taking these drugs for about two years, and they are just exhausted from taking them," he said. "They're still lifesaving drugs, but they have some very toxic side effects."

Ravinia Hayes-Cozier is executive director of the Harlem Director's Group, a coalition of AIDS service organizations that work with some 5,000 patients in Harlem. Her group helps AIDS sufferers take their medicines on the required schedules. "Many start their regimen of treatment, but they may not continue," she said. "Over time, we begin to see people falling off" their treatment schedules.

Infections Are Increasing

The success of AIDS drugs also has contributed to a growing complacency among some, especially sexually active youngsters. While deaths from HIV-AIDS have declined, new cases of infection are increasing. Half of the 40,000 new cases every year are among people under 25.

Infection rates are highest among minorities, especially blacks, who accounted for 45 percent of all new AIDS cases in 1997.

"Prevention becomes a more important tool than ever before," Ms. Hayes-Cozier said. "It's just part of Western medicine that once we find something that cures or treats a disease, we forget about prevention."

Support Services Are Strained

The fact that more people are living longer with AIDS also is placing an increasing strain on social-support networks.

Three years ago, Food & Friends served about 350 clients. Each month, about 10 percent of its clients died. "It was a tragedy, but it did mean that we had slots open" for delivering food to people, Mr. Shniderman said.

Now, however, the client list has grown to about 975 clients, and the number of clients who die is down to 3 percent per month.

"The paradox is that many clients who wouldn't have

needed our services in the past because they were deceased now still need them," Mr. Shniderman said. "They're not dying, but they're not entirely well, either."

The Tide Is Turning

Jerry should be dead.

"My doctor told me three years ago to get my will in order because I wouldn't live much longer," said the 37-year-old Mission Hills resident.

But instead of dying, the former science teacher is rewriting his resume and looking for work. Powerful new AIDS drugs called protease inhibitors have restored his weight and appetite and made him feel like new.

"I know a lot of people just like me," he said. "We don't want to be on disability anymore. We need to go back to work."

He asked that his last name not be printed to protect his chance of a job with a school or nonprofit agency.

People with AIDS in San Diego—like their counterparts nationwide—are marveling at a stunning change in the face of AIDS in recent months. Instead of dying, many people are living. They're getting out of bed, exercising, talking about returning to school, relearning a skill, buying real estate and planning retirement.

Cheryl Clark, *San Diego Union-Tribune*, February 2, 1997.

One client, who asked to be identified as "Hyde Park," has lived with HIV and AIDS since 1985. Mr. Park, 43, has lived an active life and continued working until last year, when his nagging abdominal pain was diagnosed as cancer. He spent much of last year in the hospital being treated for non-Hodgkins lymphoma.

He takes some pills three times a day, and others twice a day. "I don't think enough time has passed to really know whether these drugs will mean longer life," he said.

Public Perception

Still, reports of new medical advances have fed a public perception that the disease is all but conquered. "The word on the street is, 'The AIDS epidemic is slowing, or it's over,' just because people aren't dying as fast," Mr. Shniderman said.

AIDS fund raising is becoming more of a challenge, he said. "Public fatigue with AIDS is becoming a very real problem, because of the public perception that the AIDS epidemic is fading."

Instead, the demographics of the AIDS epidemic have shifted. It began in the United States as a disease of upper-middle-class, white, homosexual men. Homosexual men still represent 48 percent of all cases, according to the latest figures from the Centers for Disease Control and Prevention.

"But as it becomes an epidemic of the African-American minority community, some groups are showing less sympathy," Mr. Shniderman contended. "It's really a much more complicated epidemic."

Charles B. Tarver IV learned in April 1998 that he was HIV-positive. Since then, he has learned what it's like to live with a chronic illness. Initially, he felt estranged from the community.

"People are uncomfortable with any illness, not just AIDS," he said. But with the spread of AIDS to the heterosexual community has come a greater acceptance of the disease, Mr. Tarver said.

"That has leveled the playing field. Many folks all across the board are affected, and that's been the equalizer."

| *"Allegedly life-saving AIDS drugs are killing AIDS patients."*

AIDS Drugs Are Deadly

Celia Farber

Celia Farber asserts in the following viewpoint that while the drugs used to treat AIDS are helping some people, they are also killing and causing irreparable harm in others. Farber contends that the side effects from the toxic AIDS drugs are so damaging that many patients wish they were dead. She notes that the drugs are targeted at healthy people with HIV, and therefore it is easy to claim that AIDS drugs are keeping people healthy. Farber is a freelance writer who has written numerous articles on HIV/AIDS.

As you read, consider the following questions:

1. When did new HIV antibody-positive diagnoses peak, according to a study cited by Farber?
2. What was the leading cause of death for HIV-positive patients who died after taking drug cocktails, according to a hospital review cited by the author?
3. What are some other side effects experienced by patients who are taking AIDS drug cocktails, according to Farber?

The phone rang late one night and Shawn O'Hearn, 33, a San Francisco HIV prevention worker, answered it. It was an old friend, a successful dancer who, although he had tested positive for HIV, had remained in perfect health. Following the advice of the nation's leading AIDS organizations, he had begun taking a cocktail of drugs including protease inhibitors, even though he didn't have any symptoms of disease. Four weeks later, he suffered a stroke.

"I'm paralyzed, Shawn," he told O'Hearn.

He'll never dance or even walk again.

A Common Story

This is not a rare story; it is a common one in the age of AIDS drug cocktails (as the combination treatments championed by renowned AIDS researcher David Ho have become known). Such tragedies are seen as an inevitable "side effect" of a drug regimen so punishing that an entire surveillance system has been put in place to ensure that people stick to it. There are computer chips embedded in bottle caps that record the date and time of each opening. There are beepers, support groups, buddy systems, observation centers where patients take the drugs while being watched, and even groups of AIDS professionals who infiltrate people's social networks to enlist them to help promote and dispense the drugs. They call it "treatment compliance," and it has largely replaced Safe Sex as the core social imperative of the AIDS industry. The goal is to get as many HIV-positive people on the drugs as possible, whether they are sick or healthy, and to keep them on them, through debilitating ill effects, which are dismissed as a small price to pay for the benefit of lowering the amount of virus in the blood. But now, four years after the initial AIDS cocktail drug hype erupted, the utopian promise is fast turning into a nightmare.

"I started to notice that more and more friends, young people, were suffering these mysterious strokes and heart attacks," says O'Hearn, a member of the HIV Prevention Planning Council in San Francisco.

"They are listed as AIDS deaths. But those are not AIDS deaths, those are drug deaths."

San Francisco is a crucible for the new schism in the AIDS

community. The city's AIDS culture has long been characterized and dominated by the mainstream organizations which advocate drug regimens for all HIV-positive people.

One group that stands in stark contrast is ACT UP San Francisco. The group has a clientele of about 1,200 people with HIV looking for advice, support, and medical marijuana to ease their pain. "What is going on?" I ask member David Pasquarelli. "What are you seeing?" He is quiet for a moment.

"Death and deformity," he says. "Deaths from strokes, heart attacks, and kidney failure. We've lost probably half a dozen clients from sudden deaths in the past year. We've also seen at least 30 people that have distended bellies and hunchbacks from taking the drugs."

"I had a guy come in just last week and he was crying. I said, 'What's wrong?' He said that his roommate of 10 years had died suddenly, after going on cocktail therapy."

There are facts and figures, studies and counter-studies, a virtual blizzard of data that could be arranged to show any number of things. The new AIDS drugs have saved people's lives: that's one piece of truth. The new AIDS drugs have killed people: that's another. The new AIDS drugs have damaged and deformed some people so badly that although they are alive, they wish they were dead.

"Everyone keeps saying these drugs are extending lives and saving lives and we're supposed to believe it," says Pasquarelli. "I had this woman on the phone today from *HIV Plus* magazine and she said, 'Protease inhibitors are causing people to live longer,' and I said, 'No they're not. Everybody who is taking protease inhibitors is contributing to one big medical experiment. And no one knows the outcome of it.'"

Pasquarelli's group recently unearthed a 1997 study by San Francisco Health Department director Mitch Katz which exposes a shocking statistic which would appear to dispel the claim that the cocktails have caused AIDS deaths to plummet. Using stored blood samples and computer analyses, the study, published in the *Journal of AIDS and Human Retrovirology*, concluded that new HIV antibody-positive diagnoses peaked in 1982 in San Francisco—two years before HIV even had a name.

"There's a big problem in terms of looking at this as a contagious epidemic," says Pasquarelli. "HIV positive diagnoses for the past 13 years here have remained steady at 500 cases a year. People don't look at the chronology of this, or at the statistics. They just have it in their heads that these drugs save lives, and that's it." (Katz has since confirmed the group interpreted his data correctly.)

And, Pasquarelli points out, on a national level, AIDS deaths began dropping at the end of 1994, at least three years before the drugs hit the market, a fact no one disputes.

More Harmed than Helped

"There is absolutely no question whatsoever that protease inhibitors have helped people," says veteran AIDS doctor Joseph Sonnabend, co-founder of AmFAR [American Foundation for AIDS Research] now practicing in New York's Greenwich Village. "But they've probably hurt more people than they've helped. That's why it's complicated. The people for whom benefit has been proven beyond a doubt are really sick people who would have died without them three years ago. But the target population for the drug companies are the healthy people, and those people will almost certainly have their lives shortened by these drugs."

It was precisely those healthy people who were the primary target of David Ho's eradication campaign. *Time* enthusiastically exhort: "HIV-positive patients would have to start taking the drugs immediately after infection, before they realize they're sick." Ho's mantra, "Hit hard, hit early," ushered in a new machismo in AIDS treatment, where people seemed to measure their own self-worth by how long they could endure the devastating drugs.

"I have personally seen what was being called the Lazarus effect [where chronically ill people rise off their deathbeds]," says Dr. Michael Lange, chief of infectious diseases at St. Luke's-Roosevelt Hospital in New York. "But I would also say that many, many people are being badly harmed by them. Also, the regimens are so complex and hard to stick with."

"In my experience, I have seen that those who do not take any of these AIDS drugs are the ones who remain healthy and survive," says German physician Claus Koehnlein, who testified at the trial of a Montreal woman who refused to give her HIV-positive children cocktail therapy, and then in a chilling Orwellian scenario, had them taken from her and placed in a foster home where they are being forced to take the drugs.

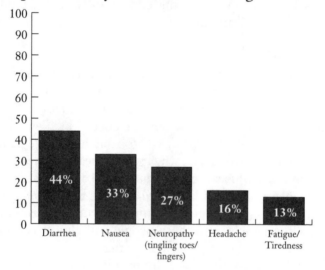

Top Five Most Common Side Effects Experienced by Antiretroviral Drug Users

Less common were vomiting (7%), rashes (5%), gas/bloating (4%), change in taste (2%), change in body shape (5%), fever (1%), and heartburn (1%). Gas/bloating and heartburn were rated the most severe by over a third of the people experiencing them.

CPS Infopack, May 1998.

"I treat the individual symptoms—the whole person, not just the virus. I treat them for whatever they are suffering from, and that's that. I have not lost a single patient in seven years and I've never used cocktail therapy."

Precisely what it means for a life to be "saved" is complicated, especially when the patient was not sick to begin with. As Koehnlein wryly commented, "If you treat completely healthy people you can claim great therapeutic success."

"The vast majority—about 75 percent—of people who go on these drugs are completely healthy," says Dr. Steven Miles, AIDS researcher and doctor at UCLA Medical Center.

"Large numbers of people are being inappropriately treated with drugs they don't need. And their lives are probably being shortened, yes."

At Lemuel Shattuck Hospital, Massachusetts, a review was done on every HIV-positive patient who died at the hospital between May 1998 and April 1999, and compared to a group of patients who died in 1991, before drug cocktails were available.

Of the 22 "post-cocktail" deaths, half died of liver toxicity from the drugs, and two more had liver toxicity listed as a secondary cause. The study concluded that liver toxicity was "now the leading cause of death among HIV-positive patients at our institution."

In other words, allegedly life-saving AIDS drugs are killing AIDS patients at this particular hospital.

Hospitals around the country are reporting radical increases in heart attacks, strokes, diabetes and other complications caused primarily by the drug's interference with the body's natural ability to metabolize fat. This is also causing the fat redistribution that leads to humpbacks and huge torso in men, and gigantic breasts in women. At the same time, fat disappears from the face, arms and legs, rendering patients stick-like. . . .

Deaths Are Not Due to AIDS

Shawn O'Hearn tested positive for HIV two years ago. He, too, went on a three-drug cocktail regimen. "I was trying to be a good little boy and make it through and stay on my regimen. I was taking almost 30 pills a day." Soon his body was covered in blisters, and he was suffering debilitating nausea. He quit the drugs after four weeks, and his health returned.

"I have many, many friends on these cocktail regimens," he says, "and some of them swear by them. But all I know is, I am seeing young people dying of very weird things that are not AIDS."

"AZT . . . given to an HIV-infected woman during pregnancy and to her baby after birth, can reduce maternal transmission of HIV by two-thirds."

AZT Reduces the Risk of Transmitting HIV from Mother to Child

National Institute of Allergy and Infectious Diseases

The National Institute of Allergy and Infectious Diseases (NIAID) supports scientists who conduct research on AIDS and other diseases. In the following viewpoint, NIAID reports that giving the AIDS drug AZT to HIV-positive women during pregnancy and childbirth, and to their newborn infants, can reduce the risk of mother-to-infant transmission of HIV by 67 percent. Although the AZT regimen is expensive, the NIAID notes that even AZT treatment of short duration substantially reduces the risk of mother-infant transmission, making the AZT regimen accessible to more women.

As you read, consider the following questions:
1. According to UNAIDS, how many children under the age of fifteen live with HIV/AIDS worldwide?
2. Which U.S. cities had the five highest rates of pediatric AIDS in 1998, as cited by NIAID?
3. Mother-to-infant transmission is estimated to cause what percentage of new HIV infections in infants and children worldwide, according to the author?

National Institute of Allergy and Infectious Diseases, "Backgrounder: HIV Infection in Infants and Children," www.niaid.nih.gov, February 2000.

The National Institute of Allergy and Infectious Diseases (NIAID) has a lead role in research devoted to children infected with the human immunodeficiency virus (HIV), the virus that causes the acquired immunodeficiency syndrome (AIDS).

NIAID-supported researchers are developing and refining treatments to prolong the survival and improve the quality of life of HIV-infected infants and children. Many promising therapies are being tested in the Pediatric AIDS Clinical Trials Group (ACTG), a nationwide clinical trials network jointly sponsored by NIAID and the National Institute of Child Health and Human Development (NICHD). Scientists also are improving tests for diagnosing HIV infection in infants soon after birth so that therapy can begin as soon as possible.

Epidemiologic studies are examining risk factors for transmission as well as the course of HIV disease in pregnant women and their babies in an era of antiretroviral therapy. Researchers have helped illuminate the mechanisms of HIV transmission as well as the distinct features of pediatric HIV infection and how the course of disease and the usefulness of therapies can differ in children and adults.

Researchers also are studying ways to prevent transmission of HIV from mother to infant. Notably, Pediatric ACTG investigators have demonstrated that a specific regimen of zidovudine (AZT) treatment, given to an HIV-infected woman during pregnancy and to her baby after birth, can reduce maternal transmission of HIV by two-thirds. Many consider this finding to be one of the most significant research advances to date in the fight against HIV and AIDS.

A Global Problem

According to UNAIDS (The Joint United Nations Programme on HIV/AIDS) and the World Health Organization (WHO), at the end of 1998, an estimated 1.2 million children worldwide under age 15 were living with HIV/AIDS. Approximately 3.2 million children under 15 had died from the virus or associated causes. The number of children who had lived with HIV from the start of the epidemic through 1997 was estimated to be 3.8 million. As HIV infection rates rise in the general population, new infections

191

are increasingly concentrating in younger age groups.
Statistics for the year 1998 alone show that
• 590,000 children under age 15 were newly infected with HIV.
• One-tenth of all new HIV infections were in children under age 15.
• Approximately 7,000 young people aged 10 to 24 became infected with HIV every day—that is, five each minute.
• Nine out of 10 new infections in children under 15 were in sub-Saharan Africa.
• An estimated 510,000 children under 15 died of AIDS-related causes, up from 460,000 in 1997.

More than 95 percent of all HIV-infected people now live in developing countries, which have also suffered 95 percent of all deaths from AIDS. In countries with the longest-lived AIDS epidemics, some doctors report that children ill from HIV occupy three-quarters of pediatric hospital beds, and childrens' life expectancy has been shortened dramatically. In Botswana, for example, because of AIDS, the life expectancy of children born early in the next decade is just over age 40; without AIDS, it would have been 70. In Namibia, the infant mortality rate is expected to reach 72 deaths per 1000, up from a non-AIDS rate of 45 per 1000.

Pediatric AIDS in the United States

The United States has a relatively small percentage of the world's children living with HIV/AIDS. From the beginning of the epidemic through the end of 1998, 5,237 American children under age 13 had been reported to the Centers for Disease Control and Prevention (CDC) as living with HIV/AIDS. Three hundred eighty-two cases of pediatric AIDS were reported in 1998. There are many more children who are infected with HIV but have not yet developed AIDS. Half of all new HIV infections reported to the CDC have been in people younger than 25. One encouraging fact is that the number of pediatric AIDS cases estimated by the CDC fell by two-thirds from 1992 to 1997 (947 to 310 cases).

The U.S. cities that had the five highest rates of pediatric AIDS during 1998 were New York City; Miami, Florida;

Newark, New Jersey; Washington, D.C.; and San Juan, Puerto Rico. The disease disproportionately affects children in minority groups, especially African Americans. Out of 8,461 cases in children under 13 reported to the CDC through December 1998, 58 percent were in blacks/not-Hispanic, 23 percent were in Hispanics, 17.5 percent were in whites/not-Hispanic, and 5.33 percent were in other minority groups.

According to 1996 data, the latest available, HIV infection was the seventh leading cause of death for U.S. children through 14 years of age. However, the CDC reported a drop of 56 percent from 1994 to 1997 in the estimated number of children who died from AIDS. New anti-HIV drug therapies and promotion of voluntary testing are having a major impact.

Transmission

Almost all HIV-infected children acquire the virus from their mothers before or during birth or through breast-feeding. In the United States, approximately 25 percent of pregnant HIV-infected women not receiving AZT therapy have passed on the virus to their babies. The rate is higher in developing countries.

Most mother-to-child transmission, estimated to cause over 90 percent of infections worldwide in infants and children, probably occurs late in pregnancy or during birth. Although the precise mechanisms are unknown, scientists think HIV may be transmitted when maternal blood enters the fetal circulation, or by mucosal exposure to virus during labor and delivery. The role of the placenta in maternal-fetal transmission is unclear and the focus of ongoing research.

The risk of maternal-infant transmission (MIT) is significantly increased if the mother has advanced HIV disease, increased levels of HIV in her bloodstream, or fewer numbers of the immune system cells—CD4+ T cells—that are the main targets of HIV.

Other factors that may increase the risk are maternal drug use, severe inflammation of fetal membranes, or a prolonged period between membrane rupture and delivery. A study sponsored by NIAID and others found that HIV-infected women who gave birth more than four hours after the rupture of the fetal membranes were nearly twice as likely to transmit HIV to their infants, as compared to women who delivered within four hours of membrane rupture.

Results of the ACTG 076 Study

More than 500 pregnant women with HIV took part in the study. Half of the mothers and babies did not take AZT. The other half of the women took AZT, and their babies were given AZT for 6 weeks after they were born.

Three of every 12 babies born to women who did not take AZT got HIV. One of every 12 babies born to mothers who took AZT got HIV.

U.S. Department of Health and Human Services, "Pregnancy and HIV: Is AZT the Right Choice for You and Your Baby?"

HIV also may be transmitted from a nursing mother to her infant. Studies have suggested that breast-feeding introduces an additional risk of HIV transmission of approximately 10 to 14 percent among women with chronic HIV infection. In developing countries, an estimated one-third to one-half of all HIV infections are transmitted through breast-feeding. The WHO recommends that all HIV-infected women be advised as to both the risks and benefits of breast-feeding of their infants so that they can make informed decisions. In countries where safe alternatives to breast-feeding are readily available and economically feasible, this alternative should be encouraged. In general, in developing countries where safe alternatives to breast-feeding are not readily available, the benefits of breast-feeding in terms of decreased illness and death due to other infectious diseases greatly outweigh the potential risk of HIV transmission.

Prior to 1985 when screening of the nation's blood supply for HIV began, some children were infected through transfusions with blood or blood products contaminated with HIV. A small number of children also have been infected through sexual or physical abuse by HIV-infected adults.

Preventing Maternal-Infant Transmission (MIT)

In 1994, a landmark study conducted by the Pediatric ACTG demonstrated that AZT, given to HIV-infected women who had very little or no prior antiretroviral therapy and CD4+ T cell counts above 200/mm3, reduced the risk of MIT by two-thirds, from 25 percent to 8 percent. In the study, known as ACTG 076, AZT therapy was initiated in the second or third trimester and continued during labor, and infants were treated for six weeks following birth. AZT produced no serious side effects in mothers or infants. Long-term follow-up of the infants and mothers is ongoing. Pediatric ACTG protocol 185 tested an AZT regimen and was reported in 1999 to have lowered MIT to about 5 percent. Combination therapies have been shown to be beneficial in the treatment of HIV-infected adults, and current guidelines have been designed accordingly. In HIV-infected pregnant women, the safety and pharmacology of these potent drug combinations need to be better understood, and NIAID is conducting studies in this area.

Researchers have shown that this AZT regimen has reduced MIT in other populations in which it has been used. Observational studies in the past few years in the United States and Europe indicate that similar reductions can be achieved by using this regimen in regular clinical care settings. In the U.S., the number of MIT-acquired AIDS cases reported to the CDC fell 43 percent from 1992 to 1996, probably because of providing AZT to HIV-infected mothers, better guidelines for prenatal HIV counseling and testing, and changes in obstetrical management.

Recent studies have shown that short regimens, too, of AZT can be beneficial in cutting back on MIT. In March 1999, researchers reported on a randomized study in Thailand on the short-term use of AZT during late pregnancy and labor in a group of non-breast-feeding women (the drug was not given to infants). They concluded that the treatment was safe and effective and can reduce the rate of MIT by 50 percent. Another recent study using a short-term AZT regimen (including post-partum) in groups of women in Ivory Coast and Burkina Faso, Africa, while limited, supported this finding.

New Prevention Trials

Following up on the success of ACTG 076, the Pediatric ACTG has begun new HIV prevention trials that build on the AZT regimen. These trials include other antiviral agents and multidrug combinations in an attempt to reduce MIT even more than that achieved by AZT alone. Also, in early 1999, a study sponsored by UNAIDS of a combination regimen of AZT plus lamivudine (3TC) in three African countries showed promising results.

The AZT regimen used in ACTG 076 is not available in much of the world because of its high cost (approximately $1000 per pregnancy, not counting counseling or testing) and logistical demands. The cost of a short-course AZT regimen is substantially lower, but is still prohibitive in many countries. International agencies are studying whether there may be innovative ways to provide AZT at lower cost, e.g., through reductions in drug prices to developing countries, partnerships with industry, etc. NIAID is pursuing a global strategy that assesses whether simpler and less costly regimens to prevent mother-to-infant HIV transmission can be effective in various settings.

Alternatives to AZT

In September 1999, an NIAID-funded study (HIVNET 012) demonstrated that short-course therapy with nevirapine lowered the risk of HIV-1 transmission during the first 14–16 weeks of life by nearly 50 percent compared to AZT in a breastfeeding population. This simple, inexpensive regimen offers a potential cost-effective alternative for decreasing mother-to-child transmission in developing countries.

The International Perinatal HIV Group reported in April 1999 that elective caesarean section delivery can help reduce vertical transmission of HIV, though it is not without risk to certain women. When AZT treatment is combined with elective caesarean delivery, a transmission rate of 2 percent has been reported.

Because a significant amount of MIT occurs around the time of birth, and the risk of maternal-fetal transmission depends, in part, on the amount of HIV in the mother's blood, it may be possible to reduce transmission using drug therapy only around the time of birth. NIAID has planned other studies that will assess the effectiveness of this approach as well as the role of new antiretrovirals, microbicides and other innovative strategies in reducing the risk of MIT of HIV.

| *"HIV-positive children who took AZT were three times more likely to develop AIDS or die by 18 months than those who did not."*

Pregnant Women and Newborns Should Not Be Treated with AZT

Susan Gerhard

AZT—a drug commonly given to HIV-positive women during pregnancy and childbirth and to their infant children—lowers the HIV transmission rate between mother and child from 25 percent to 8 percent. In the following viewpoint, Susan Gerhard contends that the risks of administering AZT outweigh the potential benefits. She asserts that for every seventeen children saved from infection by AZT, another eighty-three are being needlessly treated with a very toxic drug. Gerhard cites studies which found that children who were treated with AZT or whose mothers were given AZT during pregnancy were much more likely to sicken and die of AIDS at a young age than children who avoided exposure to AZT. Gerhard is a freelance writer who has written extensively about HIV/AIDS.

As you read, consider the following questions:
1. How do some parents avoid treating themselves and their children with AZT, according to Gerhard?
2. What were the consequences of HIV-positive women breast-feeding their infants, according to a study presented in Durban as cited by the author?

Susan Gerhard, "HIV-Positive Women Birthing Outside the System," *Mothering Magazine*, September/October 2001. Copyright © 2001 by Susan Gerhard. Reproduced with permission.

If Dana had conceived her child just one month earlier, she might have had the birth experience she had always imagined. Instead, she found herself in a cramped hospital office being informed by the Chief of Pediatric Immunology that if she decided to breastfeed her two-day-old daughter, Nia, or did not follow any other of her doctor's recommendations—he wanted to immediately give Nia a potent cell-killer, AZT—Dana would be reported for neglect, and her daughter could be taken away. Dana, a single mother, asked if she could call her family and get their advice, but the doctor told her that she had no time; she had to concede immediately or be turned over to the authorities. Three other doctors stood in the doorway in suits and lab coats as Dana, dressed only in her pajamas, was given the ultimatum. She had not slept for three and a half days.

Caught in the Dragnet

One month earlier, New York State had begun implementing a new requirement in its mandatory newborn HIV testing laws. Results of the tests would have to come back within 48 hours so that the child could be treated, and the mother "advised," before they even left the hospital. Dana (not her real name) got caught in the dragnet. Nine years earlier she had tested positive for HIV. Doctors initially told her she had too many T cells to medicate, however, and she wondered whether her HIV result might have been an error. Dana had Epstein-Barr virus, which is known to create false positives on certain HIV tests. She had remained healthy without medication, and she felt the HIV she supposedly carried might never actually make her sick. So she hadn't planned to reveal her HIV status to her doctors. But when she received a letter from the hospital informing her of changes in the law, she realized she would be one of its first targets.

Faced with the choice of either following instructions she felt would cause immediate harm to her baby or losing her child altogether, Dana did what many HIV-positive mothers feel they must do: she faked it. She agreed to follow the doctors' instructions. But when she walked down the hallway to her room, she was greeted by a lactation consultant, who apparently hadn't gotten word of Dana's predicament and was there to assist her with breastfeeding Nia. Dana didn't see any reason why she shouldn't. She just pulled the curtain around the bed and went with it.

When treating pregnant women who test positive for HIV, most physicians follow US Public Health Service guidelines, which include aggressive combinations of anti-HIV drugs during pregnancy and AZT administered intravenously during labor, followed by formula feeding and six weeks of AZT for newborns, whether or not they test positive. But many doctors, like Dana's, add their own codicil—a call to Child Protective Services if the parent doesn't comply.

Going Underground

The only way to avoid such Orwellian scenarios, many HIV-positive parents feel, is to go underground. They decline tests in 48 states where that is still allowable, look for the rare midwife knowledgeable about the reasons why a person would test HIV-positive but still be healthy, buy the AZT their doctors prescribe and flush it down the toilet, and stock formula and bottles in their cabinets while breastfeeding on the sly. They want to avoid the fate of the defiant mothers whose stories haunt the internet and talk-show circuits—Sophie Brassard in Montreal, whose two sons were taken away when she refused to treat them with AIDS drugs; Kathleen Tyson in Eugene, Oregon, who was court-ordered not to breastfeed her new son; and the Camden, UK, family who decided to flee the country to avoid having their child tested for HIV.

Dana found out that she didn't have to get tested (although Nia did) by talking to a lawyer from the HIV Law Project in Manhattan, which joins patient-advocate groups in opposing mandatory testing. She was therefore able to avoid the routine AZT drip during delivery. To avoid raising suspicion, she allowed Nia to be given three doses of AZT in the hospital, but she didn't give her any medications at home. Instead of breastfeeding, which would create breastfeeding behaviors in her baby, such as reaching for the nipple or under the shirt in public, she pumped her milk and fed Nia through a bottle. She never changed her baby's diaper in a doctor's office, where the breastfeeding tell-all, the milky orange poop, would be noticed. And she didn't let on what she had been doing when, two weeks later, her pediatrician reluctantly gave her the good news: Nia had no detectable HIV virus. The doctor admitted he hadn't wanted to tell her, because he was worried she would stop giving Nia the prescribed AZT. She did not inform him that she had already done so.

AZT Kills Babies

"Do you think that AZT had any adverse effect on your child?" I ask Kris Chmiel.

"Yes, I do," she says firmly. "She has a very enlarged cranium. That's typical of most of the AZT babies I have observed."

What she tells me next sounds like a terrible dream. "They're killing babies," she says emphatically. One young woman who came to Chmiel for counseling at the dissident AIDS activist group HEAL in Denver, had watched her child test positive for HIV shortly after being vaccinated (vaccinations can cause the HIV test to produce a false positive). The baby was put on AZT, despite the fact that the mother was HIV negative. Three months later, the baby was dead. Another mother who contacted Chmiel had a baby with hemophilia, who had received Factor 8 clotting plasma (yet another possible source of false positives). After testing positive, the baby was put on several medications and died after only five months. "That child's mother is still devastated," Chmiel says. "She believes it was the drugs that killed her son."

Celia Farber, *Mothering*, September/October 1998.

If she were to have another child, Dana says, she would not give birth in a hospital. "When the pediatrician first came in to talk to me about my test results," she remembers, "I was in a room with three other women, and he was just discussing it in front of them." Later, the hospital ended up keeping Nia an extra day after Dana herself went home. "They said it was because of jaundice," Dana says. But she believes it was to ensure the child got her AZT dose. "If I had to do it again, I would want the baby in my physical control rather than theirs."

Safety in Numbers?

Just how sound is the advice these doctors are giving? Health professionals may not volunteer the information, but studies show that AZT, the drug that was pushed on two-day-old Nia, can be extremely damaging. AZT has been shown to cause cancer and fetal deformities in animals, and the Food and Drug Administration (FDA) states that it should not be used unless the potential benefit to the fetus outweighs the potential risk.

Studies of hundreds of children who received AZT find them in worse health than their HIV-positive but less-medicated counterparts. According to one study, children born to mothers who received AZT during pregnancy showed a much higher probability of getting sick and dying by age three than children born to mothers who did not take AZT. Another study found that HIV-positive children who took AZT were three times more likely to develop AIDS or die by 18 months than those who did not. And a 1999 Columbia University observational study that adjusted for the health of the mother found children receiving AZT 1.8 times more likely to get an AIDS-defining illness or die in their first year than their counterparts who did not get the drug. Researchers have speculated that these results might depend on whether a child's "infection" occurred in utero or during delivery, but so far they have not come to an agreement.

Even in the 1994 benchmark study that opened the floodgates for AZT use among pregnant women and their newborns showed that with no drug treatment at all, only 25 percent of the women passed HIV along to their babies. Because the study, sponsored by AZT's manufacturer, showed that the drug reduced transmission from 25 percent to 8 percent, the drug has become standard treatment. But what those numbers really mean is that only 17 out of 100 children are theoretically helped by AZT. That leaves 83 percent needlessly medicated, during the most fragile moments of their lives, with a drug whose "side effects" are so debilitating it's been rejected by members of every other treatment group.

The consequences of breastfeeding, a taboo for HIV-positive mothers in the industrialized world, are no clearer. A study of 551 HIV-positive pregnant women presented in July 2000 at the XIII International AIDS Conference in Durban,

South Africa, showed that, at six months, infants who were exclusively breastfed for three months or more were no more likely to get HIV from their mothers than those who were not given any mother's milk at all.

Two Years Later

Dana's daughter, Nia, is now two years old. She drank breastmilk for four months but is now weaned and healthy, and tests for the virus still come back "undetectable." Would she have been better off if she had been taken from her mother on the second day of her life and placed on a diet of formula and AZT with foster parents? As one researcher stated, "Put simply, from a fetal viewpoint, the risk of intervention needs to be less than the risk of . . . transmission." Despite the dire predictions of the past 20 years, not every pregnant woman who is HIV-positive passes HIV along to her child, and not everyone with HIV goes on to get AIDS.

In February 2001 the National Institutes of Health (NIH) issued new treatment guidelines for adults and adolescents, the gist of which was not "hit hard, hit early" but rather, wait. NIH was worried about the toxicities of the new combination therapies, which were not curing patients as expected. NIH did not, however, revise its thinking on pregnant women or newborns taking these same toxic meds. In January 2001 the Food and Drug Administration issued a special warning to pregnant women taking nucleoside analogues ddI and d4T after three women died. The same month, the Centers for Disease Control (CDC) announced that the popular HIV-pregnancy drug nevirapine can produce liver damage severe enough to require liver transplants. CDC recommends against the use of nevirapine for health professionals who get accidental needle sticks, but still continues to recommend it for fetuses.

Periodical Bibliography

The following articles have been selected to supplement the diverse views presented in this chapter.

Susan Brink   "Improved AIDS Treatments Bring Life and Hope—at a Cost," *U.S. News & World Report*, January 29, 2001.

Shawn Decker   "Drug-Free Zone," *Poz*, March 1998.

Martin Delaney   "Whatever Became of the Cure?" *Poz*, January 2001.

Celia Farber   "Does HIV Cause AIDS?" *Mothering*, September/October 1998.

Linda C. Fentiman   "AIDS as a Chronic Illness," *Albany Law Journal*, Spring 1998.

David France   "The HIV Disbelievers," *Newsweek*, August 28, 2000.

Dave Gilden   "The Latest on Early Intervention," *Poz*, October 1998.

David Ho   "And Will We Ever Cure AIDS?" *Time*, November 8, 1999.

Sam Husseini   "The Fumento Mythology," *Extra!* November/December 1999.

John Intini   "In the Trenches," *Maclean's*, July 9, 2001.

Vickie L. Kirsten and Beverly Whipple   "Treating HIV Disease: Hope on the Horizon," *Nursing*, November 1998.

Ricki Lewis   "New Weapons Against HIV," *Scientist*, October 2001.

Bruce Mirken   "AIDS Treatment Improves Survival: Answering the 'AIDS Denialists,'" *AIDS Treatment News*, September 8, 2000.

Mark Nichols   "Rethinking AIDS: A Growing Lobby Challenges the HIV Connection," *Maclean's*, April 12, 1999.

Anne Novitt-Moreno   "AIDS: Will the Future Bring a Cure?" *Current Health*, December 1998.

Jean Scandlyn   "When AIDS Became a Chronic Disease," *Western Journal of Medicine*, February 2000.

Valendar Turner   "Do HIV Antibody Tests Prove HIV Infection?" *Continuum*, July 2001.

Tracey Walker   "Future of AIDS Treatment Rests with Slew of New Drugs," *Managed Healthcare*, November 2000.

For Further Discussion

Chapter 1

1. In 2000, there were forty-five thousand new cases of AIDS in Canada, the United States, and Mexico combined. Michael Fumento asserts that the American AIDS epidemic is over and that few Americans need to be concerned about contracting AIDS. Regina Aragón and her colleagues contend, however, that Americans should be concerned about AIDS, and indeed, many still are. After reading the viewpoints in this book, do you think the American AIDS epidemic is something Americans should worry about? Why or why not?

2. In Ian Murray's opinion, AIDS infections in Africa are increasing to the point that they are getting out of control. He believes that Americans should be concerned about the spread of AIDS in countries other than the United States. According to Tom Bethell, however, millions of deaths in Africa that have been attributed to AIDS are not AIDS-related and are actually due to common tropical diseases. Based on your reading of the viewpoints, do you believe that AIDS in Africa is a true crisis? Or, do you think that the extent has been exaggerated? Support your answer with examples from the viewpoints.

3. Robert Baker, Chantinkha C. Nkhoma, José M. Zuniga, and Rachel Cohen discuss different strategies for ending the AIDS epidemic in Africa. On what points do they agree? On what points do they differ? Which author's viewpoint most strongly influences your opinion about how AIDS in Africa should be treated? Why?

Chapter 2

1. The Centers for Disease Control and Prevention believe that the government should be given the names of people who have tested positive for HIV so that it can better track the progress of the epidemic. The San Francisco AIDS Foundation opposes names reporting and contends that the disease's progress can be tracked equally well by using coded identifiers instead of names. In your opinion, which argument is strongest? Why?

2. The theory behind mandatory partner notification—in which public health departments notify all sexual partners of a person who has been diagnosed with a sexually transmitted disease—is that when the partners of people with AIDS are treated, the spread of the disease can be controlled. Supporters of mandatory notification, such as William B. Kaliher, argue that it is nec-

essary to notify those who may have been infected so that they can protect themselves and others from becoming infected. The American Civil Liberties Union (ACLU) opposes mandatory partner notification, contending that notification does little to change risky behavior since HIV/AIDS does not have a cure. It recommends that the infected person voluntarily notify those who may have been placed at risk of infection. Based on your reading of the viewpoints, which argument do you think is strongest? Why?

3. AIDS can be passed from a mother to her newborn child during childbirth or by breast feeding. The risk of transmitting the virus from mother to child can be drastically lowered, however, through early administration of medications or by not nursing the baby. Marie McCormick believes that all pregnant women should be tested for HIV as a routine, but voluntary, part of their prenatal care. She notes that some mothers do not want to know their HIV status due to fears of discrimination and should not be forced to undergo testing. In your opinion, whose rights should be paramount—those of the mother who does not want to know her HIV status, or those of her newborn child? Please explain.

Chapter 3

1. Needle exchange programs (NEPs) are an effective means of controlling the spread of AIDS, according to Peter Lurie and Pamela DeCarlo. On the other hand, Robert L. Maginnis argues against NEPs, contending that drug addicts are not responsible enough to change their behavior in order to reduce the risk of transmitting the virus to others. Whose argument is more persuasive? Why?

2. Willard Cates Jr. maintains that condoms, when used correctly, are an effective means of preventing the transmission of HIV and other sexually transmitted diseases. According to Orestes Monzon, however, condoms have a high failure rate and are an ineffective means of protecting against HIV. Based on your reading of the viewpoints, do you think condoms protect against HIV? Support your answer with examples from the viewpoints.

Chapter 4

1. Kary B. Mullis is a respected Nobel Prize laureate who disagrees with most AIDS researchers about what causes AIDS. He believes that since there have been no studies published that can prove HIV is the cause of AIDS, it is therefore incorrect to make this assumption. Most scientists, however, have come to

accept the conclusion that HIV causes AIDS because HIV is present in every person who develops AIDS. In your opinion, does this mean that HIV causes AIDS? Explain your reasoning and support your answer with specifics from the viewpoints.

2. How do Mike Barr and Mark Schoofs differ in their viewpoints on the search for a cure for AIDS? How are they similar? Explain your answer.

3. Due to new treatments for AIDS, many people are now living longer than those who were infected at the start of the epidemic in the 1980s. Ruth Larson and Celia Farber discuss some of the effects that advances in AIDS treatments have on the lives of those who are infected. Based on these viewpoints, do you think the advances are worth the costs—financially, emotionally, and physically—to the patients? Explain your answer.

4. The National Institute of Allergy and Infectious Diseases maintains that providing AZT and other drugs to pregnant women and their newborn infants can reduce the risk of a mother transmitting HIV to her baby. Susan Gerhard contends, however, that AZT is a toxic drug that poses more risks than benefits. In your opinion, should potentially healthy babies be treated with a known toxic drug to lower the probability that they might become sick? Support your answer.

Organizations to Contact

The editors have compiled the following list of organizations concerned with the issues debated in this book. The descriptions are derived from materials provided by the organizations. All have publications or information available for interested readers. The list was compiled on the date of publication of the present volume; names, addresses, phone and fax numbers, and e-mail and Internet addresses may change. Be aware that many organizations take several weeks or longer to respond to inquiries, so allow as much time as possible.

Alive and Well AIDS Alternatives
11684 Ventura Blvd., #338, Studio City, CA 91604
(877) 411-AIDS • fax: (818) 780-7093
e-mail: info@aliveandwell.org • website: www.aliveandwell.org

Alive and Well AIDS Alternatives challenges popular beliefs and theories about HIV and AIDS. It sponsors clinical studies and scientific research in an attempt to verify the central tenets about the disease, its cause, and its treatments. The organization also provides legal and medical referrals to HIV-positive people. It publishes the book *What If Everything You Thought You Knew About AIDS Was Wrong?*

American Civil Liberties Union (ACLU)
125 Broad St., 18th Fl., New York, NY 10004
(212) 944-9800
website: www.aclu.org

The ACLU is the nation's oldest and largest civil liberties organization. It opposes mandatory partner notification of HIV status. It publishes several fact sheets including "HIV Testing of Newborns."

American Foundation for AIDS Research (AmFAR)
733 Third Ave., 12th Fl., New York, NY 10097
(212) 682-7440 • fax: (212) 682-9812
website: www.amfar.org

The American Foundation for AIDS Research supports AIDS prevention and research and advocates AIDS-related public policy. It publishes several monographs, compendiums, journals, and periodic publications, including the *AIDS/HIV Treatment Directory*, published twice a year, the newsletter *HIV/AIDS Educator and Reporter*, published three times a year, and the quarterly *AmFAR Newsletter*.

American Red Cross AIDS Education Office
1709 New York Ave. NW, Suite 208, Washington, DC 20006
(202) 434-4074
e-mail: info@usa.redcross.org • website: www.redcross.org
Established in 1881, the American Red Cross is one of America's
oldest public health organizations. Its AIDS Education Office
publishes pamphlets, brochures, and posters containing facts about
AIDS. These materials are available at local Red Cross chapters. In
addition, many chapters offer informational videotapes, conduct
presentations, and operate speakers' bureaus.

Center for Women Policy Studies (CWPS)
1211 Connecticut Ave. NW, Suite 312, Washington, DC 20036
(202) 872-1770 • fax: (202) 296-8962
e-mail: HN4066@handsnet.org
The CWPS was the first national policy institute to focus specifically on issues affecting the social, legal, and economic status of
women. It believes that the government and the medical community have neglected the effect of AIDS on women and that more action should be taken to help women who have AIDS. The center
publishes the book *The Guide to Resources on Women and AIDS* and
produces the video *Fighting for Our Lives: Women Confronting AIDS*.

Centers for Disease Control and Prevention (CDC)
National AIDS Clearinghouse
PO Box 6003, Rockville, MD 20849-6003
(800) 458-5231 • fax: (301) 738-6616
e-mail: aidsinfo@cdcnac.org • website: www.cdcnac.org
The CDC is the government agency charged with protecting the
public health of the nation by preventing and controlling diseases
and by responding to public health emergencies. The CDC National AIDS Clearinghouse is a reference, referral, and distribution service for HIV/AIDS-related information. All of the clearinghouse's services are designed to facilitate the sharing of
information and resources among people working in HIV prevention, treatment, and support services. The CDC publishes information about AIDS in the *HIV/AIDS Prevention Newsletter*, and it
includes updates on the disease in its *Morbidity and Mortality
Weekly Report*.

Family Research Council
700 13th St. NW, Suite 500, Washington, DC 20005
(202) 393-2100 • fax: (202) 393-2134
e-mail: corrdept@frc.org • website: www.frc.org

The Family Research Council promotes the traditional family unit and the Judeo-Christian value system. The council opposes the public education system's tolerance of homosexuality and condom distribution programs, which its members believe encourage sexual promiscuity and lead to the spread of AIDS. It publishes numerous reports from a conservative perspective, including the monthly newsletter *Washington Watch*, the bimonthly journal *Family Policy*, and *Free to Be Family*, a 1992 report that addresses issues such as pornography, sex education, sexually transmitted diseases, and teen sex.

Focus on the Family
8605 Explorer Dr., Colorado Springs, CO 80995
(719) 531-3400 • (800) A-FAMILY (232-6459)
fax: (719) 548-4525
website: http://harvest.reapernet.com

Focus on the Family promotes Christian values and strong family ties and campaigns against pornography and homosexual rights laws. It publishes the monthly magazines *Focus on the Family* and *Focus on the Family Citizen* for parents, children, and educators as well as the video *Sex, Lies, and . . . the Truth*, which encourages abstinence and criticizes safe-sex methods, which its members believe increase the spread of AIDS. Publications are available from its website.

Gay Men's Health Crisis
Publications/Education Dept.
119 W. 24th St., New York, NY 10011-0022
(212) 337-1950 • fax: (212) 367-1220 • TTY: (212) 645-7470
website: www.gmhc.org

Founded in 1982, the Gay Men's Health Crisis provides support services, education, and advocacy for men, women, and children with AIDS. The group produces the cable television news show *Living with AIDS* and publishes *Treatment Issues*, a monthly newsletter that discusses experimental AIDS therapies, the *Treatment Fact Sheets*, the periodical newsletters *Lesbian AIDS Project* and *Notes*, and various brochures.

Group for the Reappraisal of AIDS
1354 East Ave., Suite R-120, Chico, CA 95926-7385
(877) 256-6406 • fax: (508) 526-5944
website: www.rethinkingaids.com

Members of the Group for Reappraisal AIDS include biomedical scientists, medical doctors, and other professionals who called for an independent, scientific evaluation of traditional HIV/AIDS hypotheses. It believes HIV may be completely harmless and that AIDS is not caused by HIV but by other factors. The group publishes the newsletter *Rethinking AIDS*.

Harvard AIDS Institute
651 Huntington Ave., Boston, MA 02115
(617) 432-4400 • fax: (617) 432-4545

The Harvard AIDS Institute is a university-wide organization that promotes the understanding of HIV prevention, transmission, diagnosis, and treatment. It also works to advance AIDS education on local, national, and international levels; to provide multidisciplinary AIDS training to scientists and clinicians throughout the world; and to stimulate the development of policies and solutions that benefit those affected by the HIV epidemic. The institute publishes the newsletter *Harvard AIDS Review* twice a year.

Health, Education, AIDS Liaison
(416) 406-HEAL • fax (416) 406-HEAL
e-mail: inquiries@healtoronto.com
website: www.healtoronto.com

HEAL is a network of international chapters that challenges the validity of the traditional HIV/AIDS hypothesis and the efficacy of HIV drug treatments. HEAL believes that debate and open inquiry are fundamental parts of the scientific process and should not be abandoned to accommodate the theory of HIV. Its website provides articles that question the link between HIV and AIDS and offers information about HIV tests, AIDS in Africa, and drug treatments.

National AIDS Fund
1730 K St. NW, Suite 815, Washington, DC 20006
(202) 408-4848
website: www.aidsfund.org

The National AIDS Fund seeks to eliminate HIV as a major health and social problem. Its members work in partnership with the public and private sectors to provide care and to prevent new infections in communities and in the workplace by means of advocacy, grants, research, and education. The fund publishes the monthly newsletter *News from the National AIDS Fund*, which is also available through its website.

National Association of People with AIDS (NAPWA)
1413 K St. NW, Washington, DC 20005-3442
(202) 898-0414 • fax: (202) 898-0435
e-mail: napwa@thecure.org • website: www.thecure.org
NAPWA is an organization that represents people with HIV. Its members believe that it is the inalienable right of every person with HIV to have health care, to be free from discrimination, to have the right to a dignified death, to be adequately housed, to be protected from violence, and to travel and immigrate regardless of country of origin or HIV status. The association publishes several informational materials such as an annual strategic agenda and the annual *Community Report*.

National Institute of Allergies and Infectious Diseases (NIAID) Office of Communications
Bldg. 31, Rm. 7A-50, 31 Center Dr., MSC 2520, Bethesda, MD 20892-2520
(301) 496-5717 • fax: (301) 402-0120
website: www.niaid.nih.org
NIAID, a component of the National Institutes of Health, supports research aimed at preventing, diagnosing, and treating diseases such as AIDS and tuberculosis as well as allergic conditions like asthma. NIAID publishes educational materials, including the booklet *Understanding the Immune System* and fact sheets describing AIDS drug and vaccine development and the effect of AIDS on women, children, and minority populations.

People with AIDS Coalition (PWA)
50 W. 17th St., 8th Fl., New York, NY 10011
(212) 647-1415 • (800) 828-3280 • fax: (212) 647-1419
The People with AIDS Coalition provides a hot line for AIDS treatment information and peer counseling for individuals with AIDS. The coalition publishes *PWA Newsline*, a monthly magazine containing treatment information, news analysis, and features on people living with AIDS; and *SIDAhora*, a Spanish/English quarterly concerned with AIDS in the Hispanic community.

Rockford Institute
934 N. Main St., Rockford, IL 61103
(815) 964-5053
e-mail: rkfdinst@bossnt.com
The Rockford Institute seeks to rebuild moral values and recover the traditional American family. It believes that AIDS is a symptom of the decline of the traditional family, and it insists that only

by supporting traditional families and moral behavior will America rid itself of the disease. The institute publishes the periodicals *Family in America* and the *Religion & Society Report* as well as various syndicated newspaper articles that occasionally deal with the topic of AIDS.

Sex Information and Education Council of the United States (SIECUS)

130 W. 42nd St., Suite 350, New York, NY 10036
(212) 819-9770 • fax: (212) 819-9776
e-mail: siecus@aol.com • website: www.siecus.org
SIECUS is an organization of educators, physicians, social workers, and others who support the individual's right to acquire knowledge of sexuality and who encourage responsible sexual behavior. The council promotes comprehensive sex education for all children that includes AIDS education, teaching about homosexuality, and instruction about contraceptives and sexually transmitted diseases. Its publications include fact sheets, annotated bibliographies by topic, the booklet *Talk About Sex*, the bimonthly *SIECUS Report*, and the books *Winning the Battle: Developing Support for Sexuality and HIV/AIDS Education* and *How to Talk to Our Children About AIDS*.

Virus Myth

website: www.virusmyth.net
Virus Myth questions scientific theories that claim that HIV causes AIDS. It does not believe HIV causes AIDS or that the virus is sexually transmitted. Its website contains nearly one thousand articles that claim HIV is harmless, that AIDS is caused by toxic chemicals and drugs, and that HIV tests are worthless.

Bibliography of Books

Abbey M. Begun, Jacquelyn F. Quiram, and Nancy R. Jacobs — *AIDS*. Wylie, TX: Information Plus, 1998.

Anthony Brink — *Debating AZT: Mbeki and the AIDS Drug Controversy*. Pietermaritzburg, South Africa: Open Books, 2000.

Stuart Brody — *Sex at Risk: Lifetime Number of Partners, Frequency of Intercourse, and the Low AIDS Risk of Vaginal Intercourse*. New Brunswick, NJ: Transaction Publishers, 1997.

William A. Check — *AIDS*. Philadelphia: Chelsea House, 2000.

Jon Cohen — *Shots in the Dark: The Wayward Search for an AIDS Vaccine*. New York: WW Norton, 2001.

Peter H. Duesberg — *AIDS: Virus or Drug Induced?* Boston: Kluwer Academic Pub., 1996.

Peter H. Duesberg — *Inventing the AIDS Virus*. Washington, DC: Regnery, 1996.

Douglas A. Feldman and Julia Wang, eds. — *The AIDS Crisis: A Documentary History*. Westport, CT: Greenwood Press, 1998.

Lyn R. Frumkin and John M. Leonard — *Questions and Answers on AIDS*. Third ed. Los Angeles: Health Information Press, 1997.

Nancy Goldstein and Jennifer L. Manlowe, eds. — *The Gender Politics of HIV/AIDS in Women: Perspectives on the Pandemic in the United States*. New York: New York University Press, 1997.

Robin Gorna — *Vamps, Virgins, and Victims: How Can Women Fight AIDS?* London: Cassell, 1996.

Lawrence O. Gostin and Zita Lazzarini — *Human Rights and Public Health in the AIDS Pandemic*. New York: Oxford University Press, 1997.

Jaap Goudsmit — *Viral Sex: The Nature of AIDS*. New York: Oxford University Press, 1997.

Edward Hooper — *The River: A Journey to the Source of HIV and AIDS*. Boston: Little, Brown, 1999.

Marvin R. Kitzerow — *The AIDS Indictment*. Chicago: MRKCO Pub., 2000.

John Lauritsen and Ian Young, eds. — *The AIDS Cult: Essays on the Gay Health Crisis*. Provincetown, MA: Askleopios, 1997.

Eric K. Lerner and Mary Ellen Hombs — *AIDS Crisis in America: A Reference Handbook*. Second ed. Santa Barbara, CA: ABC-CLIO, 1998.

Christine Maggiore — *What If Everything You Thought You Knew About AIDS Was Wrong?* Fourth ed. Studio City, CA: American Foundation for AIDS Alternatives, 1999.

Susan Moore, Doreen Rosenthal, and Anne Mitchell — *Youth, AIDS, and Sexually Transmitted Diseases.* New York: Routledge, 1997.

Gabriel Rotello — *Sexual Ecology: AIDS and the Destiny of Gay Men.* New York: EP Dutton, 1997.

Gopal Sankaran, Karin A.E. Volkein, and Dale R. Bonsall — *HIV/AIDS in Sport: Impact, Issues, and Challenges.* Champaign, IL: Human Kinetics, 1999.

Joan Shelton — *Positively False: Exposing the Myths Around HIV and AIDS.* London: IB Tauris, 1998.

Barry D. Shoub — *AIDS and HIV in Perspective: A Guide to Understanding the Virus and Its Consequences.* London: Cambridge University Press, 1999.

Patricia Thomas — *Big Shot: Passion, Politics, and the Struggle for an AIDS Vaccine.* New York: Public Affairs, 2001.

Darrell E. Ward — *The AmFAR AIDS Handbook: The Complete Guide to Understanding HIV and AIDS.* New York: WW Norton, 1999.

Simon Watney — *Policing Desire: Pornography, AIDS, and the Media.* Minneapolis: University of Minnesota Press, 1997.

Index